Best Photos of the Civil War

LARRY EISINGER • EDITOR-IN-CHIEF

CONTENTS

arco publishing company, inc.

NEW YORK CITY 17, NEW YORK

Published 1961 by Arco Publishing Company, Inc.
480 Lexington Avenue, New York 17, New York

Library of Congress Catalog Card Number: 61-16881

We are gratefully indebted to the following sources
for photographs in this book: Library of Congress;
National Archives; Chicago Historical Society;
Confederate Museum; Smithsonian Institution;
Lincoln Museum; Valentine Museum; Fredericksburg
and Spotsylvania National Military Park; Mrs.
Mamie J. Chestney, Macon, Ga.; Mr. Lee Grove,
Pearl River, N. Y.; and Mr. William Lee Parker,
New York, N. Y.

ABOUT THE AUTHORS

HIRST DILLON MILHOLLEN, picture author, has, for the past thirty-five years, been associated with the Library of Congress, where he holds the position of Curator of Photographs. During his youth, he met Levin C. Handy, nephew of the most distinguished of all Civil War photographers — Mathew B. Brady. In the Handy studio in Washington he saw original negatives made during the Civil War by Brady and other photographers. This great collection is now in the Library of Congress. He has studied most of the large and small Civil War photograph collections in the country and few would dispute his position as foremost authority on the photography of the Civil War period.

Mr. Milhollen's most recent book, *Horsemen Blue and Gray*, Oxford University Press, 1960, is a pictorial history of Northern and Southern cavalry during the Civil War. His other works include *Presidents on Parade*, Macmillan, 1948, *Divided We Fought*, Macmillan, 1952, and *They who Fought Here*, Macmillan, 1959.

He writes: "My interest in the Civil War reaches back to my childhood days when old Confederate soldiers in my home town of Philmont, Va. related to me their experiences in the Confederate army, including the tales told by my uncle, Lt. Edwin Milhollen, 8th Virginia Infantry, C.S.A., who was wounded in Pickett's charge at Gettysburg."

MAJOR JAMES RALPH JOHNSON of the U.S. Marine Corps, author of text, has been collecting books and doing exhaustive research on the Civil War for more than a decade. A native of Ft. Payne, Alabama, he grew up "next door" to Civil War history and has visited most of the principal battlefields. Among his prize possessions is a 128 volume set of the *Official Records of Union and Confederate Armies*. He collaborated with Mr. Milhollen in *Horsemen Blue and Gray*, and has published a number of books, including *The Last Passenger*, Macmillan, 1956, and *Wild Venture*, Follett, 1961. In addition, he has written articles for *Leatherneck*, *Marine Corps Gazette*, and *Cavalier*.

CHARLESTON

MERCURY

EXTRA:

Passed unanimously at 1.15 o'clock, P. M., December 20th, 1860.

AN ORDINANCE

To dissolve the Union between the State of South Carolina and other States united with her under the compact entitled " The Constitution of the United States of America."

We, the People of the State of South Carolina, in Convention assembled, do declare and ordain, and it is hereby declared and ordained,

That the Ordinance adopted by us in Convention, on the twenty-third day of May, in the year of our Lord one thousand seven hundred and eighty-eight, whereby the Constitution of the United States of America was ratified, and also, all Acts and parts of Acts of the General Assembly of this State, ratifying amendments of the said Constitution, are hereby repealed; and that the union now subsisting between South Carolina and other States, under the name of " The United States of America," is hereby dissolved.

THE

UNION

IS

DISSOLVED!

A Country Divided

Long smoldering issues of the abolition of slavery and state's rights divided a once peaceful nation and led to a fratricidal conflict.

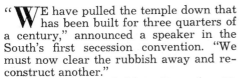

"WE have pulled the temple down that has been built for three quarters of a century," announced a speaker in the South's first secession convention. "We must now clear the rubbish away and reconstruct another."

This convention, held on December 20, 1860, in Charleston, South Carolina, pro-claimed that state an independent commonwealth. Immediately the city's enthusiasm exploded into a bedlam of ringing bells, cannon and small arms fire. Lights gleamed in windows and locomotive headlamps illuminated the streets. A Charleston *Mercury* extra appeared after the ordinance was signed.

Delegates to the secession convention addressed crowds at Charleston a few hours after South Carolina seceded from the Union. This sketch appeared in New York newspapers before the celebration had ended.

The barracks at Castle Pinckney are shown above. Obsolete, the fort symbolized U. S. authority and was seized by Confederates after Federal troops shifted to defensible Forts Moultrie and Sumter.

Lt. Adam J. Slemmer, Federal commander at Fort Pickens, Pensacola, Fla., refused to surrender and on April 11, 1861, prevented surprise seizure. Fort remained in Federal hands throughout war.

This secession decree was unanimously approved by 169 delegates, but the issues and events leading to it were complex. An immediate end to slavery had long been sought by Northern abolitionists and even by some Southerners. Most Southerners viewed slavery as a dying system. They believed it should be left to die a natural death without outside help as it had in the British Empire and in most Northern states. That view was not exclusively Southern and many influential Northerners agreed.

In spite of Abraham Lincoln's general philosophy of live-and-let-live, his election fanned the smoldering issues into flame. During the 1860 Presidential campaign, the Democratic party had split into Northern and Southern factions which enabled the Republicans, regarded by Southerners as Northern abolitionists to elect Lincoln. Within six weeks South Carolina seceded.

"We can't allow the United States to exercise authority over us any more," argued secession delegate Robert Barnwell. With the 16,000-man Federal Army scattered along frontier posts, the United

Shown below are Florida troops manning mortar at Warrington near the entrance to Pensacola Bay, which, together with Fort Barrancas, was captured by the Confederates on January 12, 1861.

Fort Pulaski (below) was seized by Georgia troops on January 3, 1861. The fort remained under the Georgia flag until April 1862, when, after heavy mortar bombardment, it surrendered to Union forces.

States was in no position to contest this stand.

On December 27, 1860, South Carolina state troops seized Castle Pinckney, a small brick fort a few hundred yards off the Charleston waterfront, and one of four U. S. fortresses in the area. Fort Johnson, a quarantine station flanking the harbor channel, was occupied on January 2. The next day Georgia troops seized Fort Pulaski near Savannah, which was followed by a seizure by Alabama of Mobile's Mt. Vernon arsenal and forts guarding Mobile Bay. Before another week was gone, U. S. forts at Appalachicola and St. Augustine, Florida had been occupied by state militia.

Near Pensacola the Federal garrison evacuated Fort Barrancas guarding the channel into Pensacola Bay, the principal U. S. naval base in those waters, and took up the defense of Fort Pickens on the Santa Rosa sand bar off the coast. Florida troops occupied deserted Fort Barrancas two days after Florida left the Union on January 10th. Nevertheless, Fort Sumter, in the middle of Charleston's harbor, remained firmly in Federal hands.

By February 4, 1861, seven Southern states—South Carolina, Mississippi, Florida, Alabama, Georgia, Louisiana and Texas—had seceded. On that date the government of the Confederate States of America was organized at Montgomery, Alabama, a temporary capital later succeeded by Richmond, Virginia.

Because of the great distances involved, the Texas delegates were unable to arrive at Montgomery in time to participate, but events in that state had not waited. Texas Governor Sam Houston, a Mexican War hero, had remarked, "They are crazy," when he heard of secession moves in the East. Few Texans held his view, however, and he was forced out of office.

On February 16th, commissioners from the "people of the state of Texas in Convention assembled" addressed a demand to the San Antonio Federal commander General Twiggs—"Deliver up all military posts and public property held by or under your control." By the time the commander arrived at his office that morning he found a thousand state troops in possession. Twiggs had little choice but to accede to the demand that he take his troops out of Texas. But as a consequence of this action he was dismissed from the Federal Army on March 1st.

On February 9, 1861, Jefferson Davis, who had been waiting to take the field with Mississippi State troops which he commanded as major general, was elected

Shown below is the surrender of General Twiggs to Texas troops in San Antonio. Chiefly settlers from the Southeast, Texans were staunch Confederates and participated in every important battle of the war.

SURRENDER OF EX-GENERAL

President of the Confederate States. He had been U. S. Secretary of War under President Pierce and lately U. S. Senator from Mississippi. Alexander H. Stevens, former staunch Unionist, was elected Confederate Vice President.

On February 18th Davis was inaugurated as provisional President; this was followed by a second inauguration as permanent President. A rousing celebration took place as the rising spirit of the new republic's citizens vented their feelings. While cannons boomed as they had in Charleston, militia companies on their way to the Florida coast gave drill displays, considered by most citizens at the moment to be the ultimate form of military preparedness.

Ironically, both Davis and Abraham Lincoln, sworn in as U. S. President on March 4, 1861, were Kentuckians by birth. A quarter century previously, Lieutenant Davis, as a U. S. Army mustering officer, had sworn in a volunteer company for the Black Hawk War whose company commander was Lincoln. Fifteen years previously the two had served in the House of Representatives together.

President Lincoln's predecessor, James Buchanan, had hesitated to take any action· which might set off the smoldering situation at Fort Sumter. He promised

Major General David E. Twiggs. "The Horse," commanded the Department of Texas at the time of secession. A native Georgian, he joined Confederates after dismissal from the U. S. Army.

The first inauguration of Jefferson Davis at the Alabama Capitol in Montgomery was described by a Washington newspaper correspondent as "The grandest pageant ever witnessed in the South."

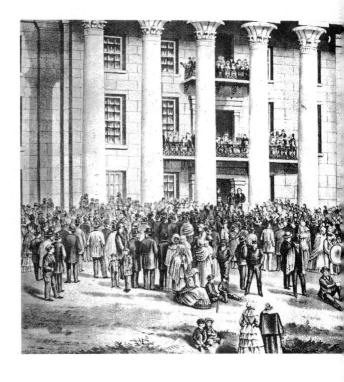

Confederate President Jefferson Davis was a West Point graduate and had served in the Mexican War.

This picture of Abraham Lincoln was taken by the famous Civil War photographer Mathew B. Brady.

Above, U. S. Army General-in-Chief Winfield Scott (standing) is shown discussing military problems involved in securing Fort Sumter at a White House meeting of President Lincoln's cabinet.

Simon Cameron (above), Lincoln's first Secretary of War, argued against attempting to hold Fort Sumter, holding that 20,000 men would be needed to defend it. He was replaced by Edwin Stanton.

Abraham Lincoln is shown riding to his inauguration with the outgoing President Buchanan. The latter tried to avoid civil conflict and was accused by both sections of maintaining a vacillating policy.

On March 4, 1861, Lincoln's inauguration as President of the United States took place on the steps of the unfinished Capitol. He pledged to execute faithfully the laws of the Union in all States.

Right, Confederate batteries at Charleston, S. C., are shown bombarding Fort Sumter in the harbor. Confederates at Fort Moultrie (on bottom at left) helped to turn back the relieving Federal fleet.

Edmund Ruffin, an elderly volunteer dressed in the uniform of the Palmetto Guards of South Carolina, is believed to have fired first shots both at Fort Sumter and later at Battle of Bull Run (Manassas).

South Carolina that he would not reprovision the Federal garrison there.

However, Lincoln looked on Fort Sumter as an opportunity to reconstitute Federal government prestige and decided to reprovision it. The Confederate Government took the position that such action constituted aggression and telegraphed the Charleston commander General Beauregard on April 11th with instructions to demand Sumter's surrender.

The surrender demand was refused by Sumter's commander. Beauregard received the following order: "Reduce the fort as your judgement decides to be most practical." Accordingly, the Confederate artillery commander alerted his batteries before midnight on April 11th. Pieces were manned and furnaces heated. At 4:30 a.m. a Confederate gun signalled the beginning of the bombardment, and Charleston rooftops were soon filled with spectators.

A Federal soldier inside Fort Sumter noted, "We all think we shall be able to stand it for about ten days. They cannot take the fort by assault unless they wish to sacrifice from three to four thousand lives. It is impossible they should enter the fort."

At six in the morning of April 12th the

Roswell S. Ripley was Confederate artillery commander at the bombardment of Fort Sumter. An Ohio native, he married and settled in Charleston. His father was then Federal Army ordnance chief.

Federal Major Robert Anderson of First U. S. Artillery was commander of Fort Sumter. A Kentuckian by birth, he remained loyal to Union. His transfer of U. S. troops to Sumter incensed the South.

relieving Federal fleet was turned back when it attempted to enter the harbor. Anderson's Federals held on for thirty-four hours, as he reported, "until the quarters were entirely burned, the main gates destroyed by fire, the gorge walls seriously injured, the magazine surrounded by flames." Only then did he accept the terms offered by General Beauregard. The fort was surrendered on Sunday, April 4th.

The Sumter action demanded quick decisions for Southern-born U. S. Army officers many of whom promptly resigned and headed for their native states. Such decisions were popular with younger officers and men, but it was believed that the General-in-Chief, Winfield Scott, would follow suit since Virginia had offered him command of its forces.

"I saw him only last Sunday," reported Lincoln's unsuccessful Presidential opponent Senator Stephen A. Douglas, "he was at his desk, pen in hand, writing his orders for the defense of the American Capital." Douglas questioned the Virginia delegation.

"I have served my country under the flag of the Union for more than fifty years," the delegates quoted Scott as saying, "and as long as God permits me to live I will defend that flag with my sword, even if my own native state assails it."

The United States was no longer united; it separated rapidly into two distinct countries with each state choosing its parent nation. Before the spring ended, U. S. population had been reduced by that of the seceding states to less than twenty million, while the Confederacy had grown to include eight million persons, one third of whom were slaves.

Many Southerners felt little concern for the fact that nearly all factories for making arms and supplying armies were located in the North.

"Our industrial pursuits have received no check," observed the Confederate President. "The cultivation of our fields has progressed," he said. "Even if we be involved in war, there should be no considerable diminution in our exports."

Southerner's took comfort in their virtual monopoly on the world's cotton supply. Responsible Confederate leaders believed that it would be only a short time until the world, and the United States, clamored for their precious commodity.

This Southern attitude was resolved quickly into a strategy of simple defense. The Confederacy would protect its borders and let the United States go its own way. "Henceforth," said Jefferson Davis, "our energies must be directed to conduct our own affairs." •

The "Star of the West" is shown approaching Fort Sumter. This merchant ship, sent to supply the defending Federal forces in the Charleston Forts, was turned back by Confederate artillery fire from shore.

Left, U. S. Army General-in-Chief Winfield Scott (seated) is shown with his staff. Although a native Virginian, this 75-year-old veteran of three previous wars chose to remain loyal to the Union.

Shown below is the gorge of Fort Sumter, taken by Charleston photographer on day of surrender to Confederates. Use of rifled cannon at bombardment ended effectiveness of masonry fortifications.

17

Call to Arms

An impatient North sent three-month volunteer recruits to the first great battle of the war.

UNITED STATES VOLUNTEERS.

THE

"UNION GUARD,"

Accepted by the Secretary of War. July 26th, '61.

This Regiment is being rapidly filled up and is under orders for Marching, within Thirty Days.

Members of this Regiment will be paid from the day of engagement.

Returned Volunteers will be allowed a liberal furlough.

Quarters and Subsistence furnished immediately upon engagement.

Uniforms will be issued as soon as ready.

Colonel P. J. JOACHIMSSEN,
Lieut. Col. pro. tem. L. M. MORRISON,
Major MAX A. THOMAN,

And the following Officers.

Capt. Arthur Brandt, Recruiting Office, No. 15 Centre St.
Capt. James H. Brennan, Recruiting Office, 7 Avenue D.
Capt. C. Wolff, Recruiting Office, 86 Walker Street.
Lieut. W. A. Thompson, Rect'ng Office, Cor. 7th Av. & 22 st.
Lieut. pro tem. Henry Herzog, Recruiting Office,
Cor. Liberty & Greenwich
Lieut. pro tem. Gustav Brandt, Recruiting Office,
Cor. Bowery & Canal Street

Headquarters 302 BROADWAY

COR. DUANE STREET.

Head Quarters, Virginia Forces,
STAUNTON, VA.

MEN OF VIRGINIA, TO THE RESCUE!

Your soil has been invaded by your Abolition foes, and we call upon you to rally at once, and drive them back. We want Volunteers to march immediately to Grafton and report for duty. Come one! Come ALL! and render the service due to your State and Country. Fly to arms, and succour your brave brothers who are now in the field.

The Volunteers from the Counties of Pendleton, Highland, Bath, Alleghany, Monroe, Mercer, and other Counties convenient to that post, will immediately organize, and report at Monterey, in Highland County where they will join the Companies from the Valley, marching to Grafton. The Volunteers from the Counties of Hardy, Hampshire, Randolph, Pocahontas, Greenbrier, and other Counties convenient, will in like manner report at Beverly. And the Volunteers from the Counties of Upshur, Lewis, Barbour, and other Counties, will report at Philippi, in Barbour County. The Volunteers, as soon as they report at the above points, will be furnished with arms, rations, &c., &c.

Action! Action! should be our rallying motto, and the sentiment of Virginia's inspired Orator, "Give me Liberty or give me Death," animate every loyal son of the Old Dominion! Let us drive back the invading foot of a brutal and desperate foe, or leave a record to posterity that we died bravely defending our homes and firesides,—the honor of our wives and daughters,—and the sacred graves of our ancestors!

[Done by Authority.]

M. G. HARMAN, Maj. Comm'g
at Staunton.
J. M. HECK, Lt. Col. Va. Vol.
R. E. COWAN, Maj. Va. Vol.
May 30, 1861.

During the Civil War 2,500,000 men served in the Union Army. Federal conscription began in March, 1863; 170,000 men were subsequently drafted.

About a million men served in the Confederate Army during the war. Conscription began in April, 1862, and all men between 17 and 50 were eligible.

Members of Company D, 1st Rhode Island Infantry are shown at Camp Sprague, near Washington, shortly after their enlistment. These men participated in the Battle of Bull Run (Manassas) a few weeks later.

THE day after Sumter's surrender President Lincoln asked state governors to provide him with 75,000 militia troops. The purpose, as Lincoln stated, was to repossess installations seized from the Union. Although there was prompt and spirited response by the northern states, Lincoln's request was refused by Arkansas, Kentucky, Maryland, Missouri, North Carolina, Tennessee and Virginia. Delaware's governor pleaded lack of authority.

Initially, Virginia refused to secede, but on the day after Lincoln's call for troops, a secession ordinance was adopted and prepared for popular vote. The ordinance was ratified as soon as voters were able to express themselves by ballot, but Virginia authorities did not await election results.

Four days after Lincoln's call, Virginia ordered seizure of the U. S. Arsenal at Harper's Ferry and the Norfolk Navy Base. The Harper's Ferry garrison commander, learning of approaching Virginia troops during the night of April 18th, fired the arsenal before evacuation. "In ten minutes, or less," he reported, "both of the arsenal buildings, containing nearly 15,000 arms,

together with the carpenter's shop were in complete blaze." The Federal troops marched all night to Carlisle Barracks, Pennsylvania.

Soon there were indications that groups of Southern sympathizers in Maryland intended to prevent Federal troop movements through that state. Bridges were burned and threats made.

"Every effort," telegraphed Baltimore's anxious mayor to Lincoln, "is being made to prevent parties leaving the city to molest troops marching to Washington. Baltimore seeks only to protect herself."

The 6th Massachusetts Militia, on its way to Washington, was only a short distance between Baltimore's rail terminals, however, when "they were furiously attacked by a shower of missiles, which became faster as they advanced," according to Colonel Jones, the Federal commander. "They increased their steps to double-quick which seemed to infuriate the mob. Pistol shots were numerously fired into the ranks, and one soldier fell dead."

The soldiers were ordered to return the fire and although the mayor, who escorted the Federal column, begged the com-

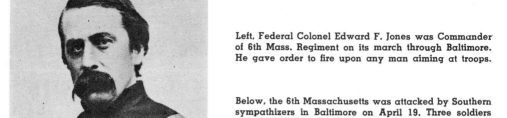

Left, Federal Colonel Edward F. Jones was Commander of 6th Mass. Regiment on its march through Baltimore. He gave order to fire upon any man aiming at troops.

Below, the 6th Massachusetts was attacked by Southern sympathizers in Baltimore on April 19. Three soldiers were killed, 40 wounded, and one citizen was killed.

Shown below with his staff is Brigadier General Irwin McDowell (center looking left), who commanded the Federal army at the Battle of Bull Run. He was routed by Stonewall Jackson at Manassas rail junction.

Above left, Federal First Lieutenant Roger Jones of the U. S. Army's Mounted Rifles commanded the U. S. Armory at Harper's Ferry (right) when Virginia state forces attacked it. He destroyed the arsenal to prevent capture of its arms and was congratulated by the Secretary of War for "judicious conduct."

mander to order a cease fire, he seized a musket from one of the men and shot a rioter himself.

By early summer the North became impatient. Soldiers, recruited with the expectation of action on the battlefield, saw little evidence of it. Three-month enlistments were expiring. Pressured by newspapers and politicians, Lincoln reluctantly ordered his ill-prepared army to move south.

The Federal army was led by Brigadier General Irvin McDowell, whose aptitude for the ingestion of food eclipsed, in the eyes of critics, his military talent. McDowell directed troop formations toward Manassas Junction, a rail fork twenty miles southwest of the capital, and, with picnic baskets, the Washington populace journeyed down in carriages to watch the battle.

It took two days to make such a movement, and, considering the inexperience of new commanders in marching large groups over narrow roads, it was well done.

Confederates took position along the southern bank of a creek named Bull Run. McDowell planned to feint at their front

Federal General McDowell set up headquarters here at Centreville, Virginia, two days before the Battle of Bull Run. He struck the Confederate left rather than right because of latter's rough terrain.

Confederate General Pierre Gustave Toutant Beauregard, a West Point graduate, was the commander of Southern forces at the Battle of Bull Run.

Above, Federal soldier guards Stone Church at Centreville, three miles northeast of the Stone Bridge. Federal reserves were stationed here during battle and fields were used for bivouac.

Confederate Brigadier General Edmund Kirby Smith brought three fresh regiments from the Shenandoah Valley and caused the first setback to the Federal forces during the Battle of Bull Run.

while sending a flanking force upstream to his right. This force would sweep in behind Confederate lines.

The plan was a good one. Union troops struck the Confederate left at ten in the morning, and outnumbered Confederates were driven back. A British reporter on the hills to the north quoted a woman spectator holding an opera glass exclaiming, "That is splendid. Oh, my! I guess we will be in Richmond tomorrow."

By noon the battle had become a confused faltering struggle. Later, scattered Federal soldiers began slipping to the rear. Gradually the entire Federal army became swept with panic. A rout developed, urged on by Confederate artillery which wrecked a wagon on Cub Run bridge, blocking the main road to the rear.

"The men are a confused mob, utterly demoralized," ranted McDowell. Retreating Federal cavalry were mistaken for charging Confederate horsemen, and when the latter finally arrived in pursuit they found the woods and fields crawling with Federal soldiers streaming toward Washington. A pistol-carrying New York Congressman was among the captured. Casualties to Federal forces totalled 2,700; Confederates—1,900.

Shown above are ruins of Henry House in center of battlefield south of Bull Run Creek. Confederate troops captured artillery of the Federals, who began their retreat here.

These Federal 11th New York Zouaves were captured by Confederates at Bull Run and confined here at Castle Pinckney in Charleston harbor. They were exchanged in 1861.

Stunned by the Federal retreat, Washington prepared to defend itself. There was little danger from Confederate attack, for the Confederates were as disorganized by their victory celebrations as were the Federals by defeat.

The fight had evaporated from many of the Federal 3-month volunteers. However, "Bull Run," called by Southerners "First Manassas," had a lethargic effect on many Southerners, convinced that one "Reb" was worth ten "Yankees." ●

Peninsula Campaign

McClellan's army attacked up the Peninsula, which lies between the York and James Rivers, but did not succeed in capturing the rebel Capital.

Federal Major General George D. McClellan, called "Napoleon of the West," had chased Lee's forces from West Virginia at beginning of war. He seemed answer to Lincoln's search for capable army head.

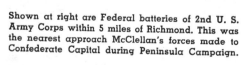

Shown at right are Federal batteries of 2nd U. S. Army Corps within 5 miles of Richmond. This was the nearest approach McClellan's forces made to Confederate Capital during Peninsula Campaign.

THE day after the Battle of Bull Run, President Lincoln telegraphed General McClellan in West Virginia. "Circumstances make your presence here necessary —come hither without delay." The President appointed him General-in-Chief.

An average of 10,000 new Federal soldiers arrived in the Washington area each month, and the magnetic young McClellan displayed a remarkable talent for organizing and training them. The defeat at Bull Run was momentarily forgotten as the military preparation of Federal soldiers absorbed his attention. The calm atmosphere along the Potomac was broken by a new Federal excursion in late October near Washington at Ball's Bluff. It turned into another Federal disaster.

Meanwhile, McClellan had been advocating a plan to take Richmond by attacking up the peninsula between the York and James Rivers southeast of the city, but the President and Secretary of War expressed reservations. Intelligence reports revealed a disturbing new weapon in Confederate hands, the former U.S.S. *Merrimac*, scuttled and sunk by evacuating Federals. The Confederates had raised her, clad her sides in iron armor. It was believed that the ship might be used to bombard Washington, but in early March, 1862, the ex-*Merrimac*, now re-christened C.S.S. *Virginia*, was held to a draw in a fight with the Federal ironclad *Monitor*. With this threat countered, McClellan loaded his army aboard 400 transports and supply ships in mid-March, and sailed down Chesapeake Bay for debarkation at Fort Monroe, on the sea channel of Hampton Roads, Virginia.

Federals used "Quaker guns," or logs mounted and painted to resemble cannon to deceive their Confederate opponents into thinking that Union forces possessed more artillery than they actually had.

Shown below is the Federal 96th Pennsylvania Infantry, which participated in many important engagements during the campaign. Here the men are seen training at Camp Northumberland near Washington.

During the campaign, the 27th New York Infantry, shown here drilling before the earthworks of Ft. Lyon, Va., defended perimeter around U. S. Capital. This regiment had 60% casualties later at Fredericksburg.

Right, this 32-pounder Federal gun at Ft. Woodbury, Arlington, Va., was one of many such pieces used for the defense of Washington. Officer held thumb over vent in rear to prevent influx of oxygen while charge was being rammed.

Although a few breech-loading (loaded from rear) cannon were used in the Civil War, they were not popular since they leaked powder gases at the breech. Number 3 cannoneer (right) is poised to pull lanyard upon the command "fire."

Shown above is the headquarters of Confederate General Magruder at Yorktown, Va. The Confederate defense by 15,000 men against McClellan's 100,000-man army was directed from this house.

Confederates were able to use many existing earthworks constructed at Yorktown by British General Cornwallis before his surrender during the American Revolution. These howitzers held for a month.

Shown below is Federal mortar battery No. 4 at Yorktown. Ten 13-inch mortars were set up a mile from Confederate defenses. None of the batteries (15 in all) fired a shot before evacuation by Confederates.

Another view of Federal mortar battery No. 4 is shown above. These weapons, heaviest to be used in siege operations until 1862, were landed in late April and were ready to fire within a week.

Shown above is an encampment, at White House, Va., of 40,000 troops of the Army of the Potomac. This camp was set up, during the build-up for the campaign, on land belonging to the son of Gen. Lee.

The Confederate commander in the Shenandoah Valley, Stonewall Jackson, was engaged in threatening Washington and in preventing Federal troops from reinforcing McClellan. Jackson was an admirer of Napoleon's abilities to move and mass quickly, and he believed in attacking in adroit thrusts and parries. In March with 18,000 Confederates behind him, Jackson engaged his cavalry with Federal forces in Kernstown, Virginia, and followed with his infantry. However, Federal General Banks then marched up with 20,000 troops and drove Jackson away. However, the Confederate leader quickly turned this setback into an advantage. Jackson's opponents were held in the Valley, and substantial Federal forces, halted at the Rappahannock River were unable to assist McClellan.

Jackson continued parrying. He swept through western passes and defeated Fremont's force of 15,000 troops at Staunton, Virginia, and returned to rout General Banks from the northern Shenandoah.

"Crawling like a snail," as impatient Northern papers described him, McClellan worked up the Peninsula. Confederates had built a defense line across the Peninsula from Yorktown to the James River, and McClellan spent two tedious months setting up siege guns. On May 4th, when the firing was scheduled to begin, McClellan found that the Confederates had abandoned the line during the night and dropped back to Williamsburg.

The next day McClellan's forces pursued the Confederates, but soon became scattered in the Virginia swamps. "I found everybody discouraged, officers and men," McClellan wrote his wife, "no system, no

cooperation, no orders given. As soon as I came upon the field the men cheered like fiends, and I saw at once that I could save the day." The Federal advance struck the Confederate rear guard at Williamsburg in a sharp fight. "We have given them a tremendous thrashing," said McClellan.

Criticized for the withdrawal up the Peninsula, Confederate Commander Joseph Johnston explained, "I proposed that all our available forces should be united near Richmond to fall upon McClellan when the Federal army was expecting to besiege only the troops it had followed from Yorktown."

As McClellan's army edged within sight of Richmond's church steeples, Johnston launched the first major battle of the campaign, that of Fair Oaks.

Confederate units straggled into the Battle of Fair Oaks piecemeal on May 31st, and Johnston was seriously wounded before nightfall. On the evening of June 1st, Confederates drew back after suffering a loss of 6,000 men, a thousand more than Federal casualties.

In the Shenandoah Valley, Stonewall Jackson rested after pushing Banks' Federals back into Maryland. He loaded huge amounts of captured arms and ammunition onto wagon trains and sent them south. An army of 20,000 Federal troops from the Rappahannock then marched west to unite with Fremont and Shields, but while holding Fremont at bay, Jackson drove off Shields at Cross Keys and Port Republic, and found himself securely in possession of the upper Shenandoah.

Johnston's successor, Robert E. Lee, who focussed his attention on strengthening the fortifications at Richmond, ignored criti-

Shown at left is a scene of White House Landing on the Pamunkey River, twenty-five miles northeast of the Confederate Capital. This Federal supply base had to be abandoned by Union forces during the Seven Days Battles.

Members of the 5th New Hampshire, 64th New York, and Irish Brigade are shown at work on the "Grapevine" bridge across the Chickahominy River. The bridge was completed on May 29, enabling reinforcements to rush across to Fair Oaks.

General Joseph E. Johnston was commander of the Confederates before Richmond. He was offered command of the Union Army in April, 1861, but this native Virginian refused it and joined Confederates.

Federal observation balloon "Intrepid" is shown being filled with hydrogen from the storage balloon below it. Federal balloons provided accurate reconnaissance of Confederate battlefield movements.

Federal ground crews pay out handling lines during a balloon ascension. Telegraph wires were run up to an operator in basket to allow instant reporting by Professor T. S. C. Lowe (inset), head of balloon program.

cism from impatient Southerners hoping for a bold stroke. Learning that a Federal corps was isolated north of the Chickahominy River, Lee, amidst much fanfare, sent reinforcements to Jackson in the Shenandoah, while Jackson rushed to a war conference at Richmond.

Jackson's plan was to strike the Federal right and other Confederate divisions would follow. Unfortunately for Lee, Jackson was unable to get his men into position on the morning of June 26th. Nevertheless, that afternoon a portion of the Confederate force began the attack. Charging an unsuspectedly fortified position, twenty-one

Confederate regiments met withering fire. The 44th Georgia lost all its officers and a handful of men limped away. On June 27th Jackson arrived and led the second of the Seven Days Battles, as they came to be called. At dusk the Federal line broke and McClellan's men streamed across the Chickahominy River. McClellan changed his base to the south side of the Peninsula, on the James River. Displaying his ability for organizing an orderly movement of troops, the Federal commander led his army of nearly 100,000 men through White Oak Swamp to the natural defensive position at Malvern Hill, where artillery could

Gibson's Battery of the 3rd U. S. Artillery is shown in reserve at the Battle of Fair Oaks. Separated by the Chickahominy River from the battle, these crews of Companies C and G had no opportunity to assist.

This Confederate 12-pound-er napoleon howitzer was captured by Federal forces on the Peninsula. This model probably produced more artillery-fire casualties in both armies than any other cannon used in the war.

Seated with staff, Federal General George Stoneman (right) hands note to orderly. Before the Battle of Fair Oaks, Stoneman's cavalry successfully raided Confederate railroads and fought Stuart's cavalry at Hanover Court House, north of Richmond.

Below is an on-the-spot drawing made of the Battle of Glendale, June 30, 1862, one of the Seven Days Battles. These Federal soldiers of Brigadier General Philip Kearney's division are engaged in "bushwacking" as this type of fighting was called.

This scene is of Savage Station on the Richmond and York River Railroad. The Federal guard held off attacking Confederates here on June 29, 1862, long enough to prevent Lee from intercepting Union Army.

This on-the-spot drawing, by A. R. Waud, shows Federal forces withdrawing before daylight on Sunday, June 29. Commissary stores and forage were set afire and artillery covered the retreat of 16th N. Y. Inf.

On June 28, Federals evacuated their base at White House and burned this railroad bridge across Pamunkey. That night full trains were run off bank into river at full throttle to prevent rebel seizure.

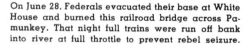

sweep Confederate lines approaching over open fields.

Lee waited for two days in order to make certain of McClellan's maneuver. Then he struck as quickly as his columns could be gathered. His aim was to decimate the Union guard at Savage Station, thus permitting a flank attack between White Oak Swamp and Malvern Hill.

However, this attack was late. During afternoon, the Confederate thrust was successfully parried, and the Union rear guard escaped.

The forces of Confederate Generals Longstreet and A. P. Hill, however, were in position to strike the Federal flank. Deciding not to await Jackson, Longstreet struck at Frayser's Farm. Before Confederate reinforcements could arrive, the

Federal Colonel James E. Childe and officers of the fourth Pennsylvania Cavalry are shown above. Mc-Clellan's horsemen spent long hours fighting rear guard actions during the withdrawal of Federal forces.

fight was over and the Federal army slipped past to Malvern Hill.

The Malvern Hill battle turned out to be Lee's greatest tactical mistake. The hill was flanked by swampland, and the James River allowed close approach by Federal gunboats. Assuming that the Federal army was in retreat, Lee threw his units toward Malvern Hill on July 1st as fast as they could come up. Then the 250 Federal artillery pieces on the hill opened in support of counter-charging Federals. Confederates reeled back, leaving 5,000 casualties on the slopes. Although repulsed, Southerners found they had gained their main objective, relief of Richmond.

The Seven Days Battles were over. By mid-August the Federal army was marching back down the Peninsula. •

The drawing was made during the Battle of Malvern Hill, July 1, 1862. Federal General Fitz John Porter's 5th Corps are shown firing on Confederates moving across open ground in distance.

North of the Potomac

The battles of Second Manassas and Antietam proved indecisive.

A FTER the Union threat to Richmond
was removed by the Seven Days
Battles in the summer of 1862, the Confederacy abandoned the defensive philosophy of fighting only when attacked. A
decision was made to carry the war to
Northern soil. The Federal struggle in the
East wavered momentarily, and no novel
and imaginative Union strategy was forth-
coming.

Soon after Malvern Hill, Lincoln brought
Major General Henry Wager Halleck to
Washington as General-in-Chief in place
of McClellan who was ordered to send his
soldiers down to Major General John Pope.
In early August Pope moved 50,000 Fed-

Confederate General Robert E. Lee resigned from
U. S. Army to head the Army of Northern Virginia.

J. H. Deveraux, Superintendent of the Orange and Alexandria R.R., is seen atop bank supervising repair of the railroad.

Below right, Federal workers are shown repairing railroad near Catlett's Station after Jackson's raiders wrecked it.

This wood-burning Federal locomotive, the "General Haupt" was the pride of the United States Military R.R.

These young Federal soldiers at Manassas Junction are surveying damage caused by Jackson's raiders. Although reserve supplies worth a million dollars were destroyed here, the Union Army quickly recovered.

Shown above is the Federal supply depot at Manassas Junction after its destruction by Jackson.

eral troops south of the Rappahannock's headwaters. His advance, led by Banks, struck Lee's advance under Stonewall Jackson at Cedar Mountain, 35 miles west of Fredericksburg. The Federal soldiers charged, suffered heavy losses, and recoiled. Left in possession of the battlefield, Jackson refused to engage the approaching Federal main force with only half as many Confederates, and decided to move back south of the Rapidan.

Lee rushed preparations to strike before McClellan's reinforcements could join Pope. Taking a bold risk, Lee sent Jackson's corps to the west with instructions to march around Pope's army and fall on his

Federal engineers are shown righting a capsized locomotive. Jeb Stuart's cavalry threw a switch at Bristoe's Station and this locomotive jumped the track.

Federal commanders were forced to detach sizable forces from front-line units to guard the military railroads in Virginia from Confederate cavalry raiders.

supply base at Manassas Junction, while Lee hurried the bulk of the Confederate army northward.

On August 25th, Jackson's men marched 25 miles. "Many of them had no rations, and subsisted upon the green corn gathered along the route," remembered one Confederate, "yet their indomitable enthusiasm and devotion knew no flagging." The next day they walked another 25 miles to the Orange and Alexandria Railroad, picking up Jeb Stuart's cavalry during the day.

At Manassas Junction, Jackson scattered the guarding Federal brigade. After stuffing empty blanket rolls, the Confederates set fire to the vast supply depot,

and prepared to receive Pope's advancing army on the familiar Manassas battlefield. Jackson was in luck, for a Confederate cavalryman rode in with a captured order from Pope revealing Federal concentrations at Manassas. This intelligence enabled Jackson to position his men, and on the afternoon of August 28th he struck Pope's men marching along the turnpike toward Manassas Junction.

That night it seemed to Pope that Jackson was retreating toward the western gaps. Jackson's men, however, were taking position behind a railroad embankment where they fought off Pope's attack the next day while waiting for Lee's rein-

Above, this Federal bivouac was pitched by Pope's army of Virginia below Cedar Mountain, five miles southwest of Culpeper, Va.

These two Northern photographers are camped with their equipment at Bull Run Creek prior to the battle of Second Manassas.

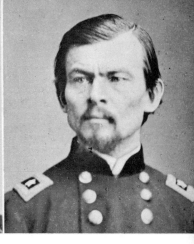

Confederate Brigadier General M. D. Corse commanded Confederate units at Second Bull Run and later at Battle of Antietam.

Federal Major General Franz Sigel took command of General Fremont's army corps prior to the Battle of Cedar Mountain.

Above left, this photo, made on August 9, 1862, shows napoleon howitzers being moved to the front a few hours before the Battle of Cedar Mountain. During the battle 2,000 Federal and 1,300 Confederate soldiers were casualties.

Shown at right are fugitive slaves retreating with Pope's army. A few days before the Battle of Cedar Mountain, Federal commanders were ordered to employ Negroes for various military purposes and pay them suitable wages.

forcements. Still confused about the true situation, Pope sent Fitz John Porter around to attack Jackson's right flank.

Upon his arrival, Porter was confronted with Confederate General Longstreet's corps, which had just approached. Porter spent the afternoon fighting Longstreet. On August 30th, Pope ordered his men after "retreating" Confederates. This time opponents were on opposite fields from those of the previous summer during the First Battle of Bull Run.

Longstreet's artillery shot down the axis of the Federal lines, and when that shelling had done its work, Longstreet sent his infantry forward to destroy the Federal left.

Completely baffled, Gen. Pope gathered his army during the night and straggled them off toward Washington, turning back 30,000 Federal reinforcements on the way. Pope arrived in Washington to find himself replaced by McClellan. "Again I have been called upon to save the country," the temporarily redeemed "Little Mac" said.

Robert E. Lee was now in a position considerably changed from that of two months before, when the Northern army besieged the Confederate capital. Second Manassas had driven the Federals behind the defensive perimeter of Washington. The road to Maryland was open, and victory there could be decisive.

Major General John Pope was in command of all Federal forces at the Battle of Second Manassas.

Shown below is a pontoon bridge laid by Federal troops across the Potomac at Berlin, Maryland.

Drawing below depicts Federal retreat from Battle of Second Manassas, Saturday, August 30, 1862.

On Sept. 15, 1862, Jackson captured Harper's Ferry (above right) and quickly rejoined Lee at Manassas.

"We had the most brilliant prospects the Confederates ever had," wrote General Longstreet. "We then possessed an army, that, if kept together, the Federals would never have dared attack." Eager to head north, Longstreet reasoned that his men "could not starve at that season so long as the fields were loaded with roasting corn."

After resting his men for one day, Lee headed his battle-worn army north. On September 5th Stonewall Jackson waded the Potomac with an old lady there singing "Lord bless your dirty, ragged souls!"

Dividing his force in the face of McClellan's superior army marching up from Washington, Lee instructed Jackson to capture Harper's Ferry. Jackson took 12,000 Federal prisoners and 73 cannon. On September 14, 1862, a part of Lee's force fought the Battle of South Mountain, astride the Federal approach route. It was a battle of "extraordinary illusions and delusions," according to Confederate D. H. Hill, the blocking commander, "the Confederates deluded the Federals into the belief that the whole mountain was swarming with rebels."

The night after the Battle of South Mountain Lee concentrated his force west of Antietam Creek, a position including the town of Sharpsburg, Maryland. On

Shown above is Lincoln at Antietam with Allan Pinkerton (left) and General John A. McClernand (right).

Right, Company G of the Twenty-Second New York State Militia is shown parading at Harper's Ferry.

Right, these men (35th New York Infantry) fought Lee's forces at the Battle of South Mountain, Maryland.

Above, rifled Parrott guns opened on Confederate lines at Antietam after dawn on Sept. 17, 1862.

Under flag of truce, stretcher parties of both armies worked alongside picking up their wounded.

Below, rebel Lieutenant Gen. A. P. Hill saved Lee's army at Antietam when he arrived during battle.

September 17th, aided by the capture of one of Lee's orders, McClellan opened battle with a superiority in men of two to one, but was unable to dislodge the Confederates in the bloodiest single day's battle of the war. Throwing in reserves without hesitation, Lee straightened his lines as Federal pressure bent them, while the cautious McClellan held back a large number of reserves which otherwise would probably have been decisive.

One civilian followed along after the Federal advance in the center that day. "The Confederates had gone down as the grass falls before the scythe. They were lying in rows, like the ties of a railroad; in

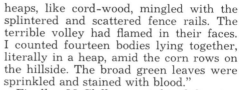

These dead of Stonewall Jackson's corps were killed at Antietam along the Hagerstown turnpike by Hooker's artillery loaded with canister shot.

heaps, like cord-wood, mingled with the splintered and scattered fence rails. The terrible volley had flamed in their faces. I counted fourteen bodies lying together, literally in a heap, amid the corn rows on the hillside. The broad green leaves were sprinkled and stained with blood."

Finally, McClellan sent his left wing across Antietam Creek. As General Burnside wrestled the Confederate defenders off the hill and into Sharpsburg, General A. P. Hill's men force-marched in from the Harper's Ferry fray. They deployed on the run, led by their bearded commander in a red shirt. Contesting lines slowed as dusk approached.

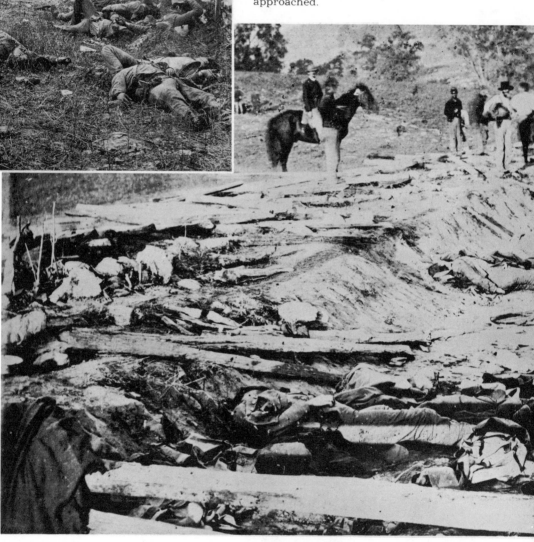

Casualties were so heavy at Antietam that September 17, 1862, was termed the "bloodiest day of the war."

After dark, litter parties picked out the wounded from 24,000 casualties scattered over three miles. The next day, as Federal reinforcements continued arriving, Lee, with no prospect of reinforcement, held his ground. That night the Confederates forded across the Potomac River and began marching south.

In Washington President Lincoln deemed the moment appropriate for issuing his famous Emancipation Proclamation which he had been preparing for weeks. From January 1, 1863, he announced, all slaves in rebel territory were free. Foreign intervention on the side of the Confederacy was discouraged, for in world opinion the American Civil War had become a freedom crusade.

The day after Antietam a Northern reporter noted that "a change had come over the army. The complacent look which I had seen upon McClellan's countenance on the 17th, as if all were going well, had disappeared. There was a troubled look instead —a manifest awakening to the fact that his great opportunity had gone by. Lee had slipped through his fingers."

A month passed before McClellan got his 115,000 men across the Potomac to pursue the Confederates. Lincoln, whose patience was exhausted, personally drafted an order relieving McClellan of his command. •

This sunken road at Antietam, filled with Confederate dead, was called "Bloody Lane." Here, a column of troops was hit by Union artillery fire.

After the battle this train of Federal army wagons was photographed. The Federal army was too crippled and disorganized to pursue Lee.

Struggle for Virginia

The Federal disasters at Fredericksburg and Chancellorsville gave a ray of hope to the Confederacy.

STONEWALL JACKSON

48

AMBROSE BURNSIDE, McClellan's successor, wasted no time after Lincoln selected him to command the Federal Army of the Potomac. In two days his advance elements reached a point overlooking Fredericksburg from the north bank of the Rappahannock River. There Burnside waited impatiently while pontoniers bridged the river. The hills behind the town were crawling with Confederates. The choice of Fredericksburg as a crossing site was a poor one. Federal cannon swept the movement from the north bank, but the town's buildings provided cover for Confederate sharpshooters, and the open plain separating the town and the ridge behind it, Marye's Heights, was ideal for emplacement of rebel artillery.

Lee placed cannon atop Marye's Heights and put successive lines of infantry on the slopes, beginning at a stone wall along the bottom. On the night of December 10th, Burnside laid his pontoon bridges while snipers harassed his engineers. Two days later, Federals crossed in strength, Sumner on the right, Franklin on the left and Hooker in the center.

The next morning the town and plain were hidden by fog. When it cleared Confederates saw 40,000 blue-clad enemy targets before them. A Confederate artilleryman told his commander, "We cover that ground now so well that we will comb it as if with a fine tooth comb. A chicken could not live on that field when we open."

At noon the Federal charge began. "Oh, great God," gasped Federal General Darius Couch to a friend as they watched, "Our men!" He wrote later, "I remember that the whole plain was covered with men, prostrate and falling." About 12,000 Federal and 5,000 Confederate troops were shot

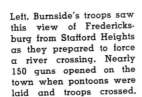

Wooden pontoon boats were used extensively at Fredericksburg by the advancing Federal army. Soldiers rowed across the river under fire at Franklin's Crossing and established a bridgehead there.

Left, Burnside's troops saw this view of Fredericksburg from Stafford Heights as they prepared to force a river crossing. Nearly 150 guns opened on the town when pontoons were laid and troops crossed.

A near disaster occurred on this bridge when a band played a marching song. Men fell into step causing structure to weaken from their cadence. Quickly the commander stopped music and the bridge was saved.

Federal Major General Andrew A. Humphreys led one of the last Union charges against Marye's Heights at Fredericksburg, and received a brevet promotion "for gallant and meritorious services."

down before the attack stopped. The next day when another attack was formed, Federal soldiers slipped from ranks to find refuge among the dead. Adamantly, Burnside wanted to make another attempt with himself at the head of 17 regiments. "I came to the conclusion that Burnside was fast losing his mind," said General Franklin, who helped dissuade him. Reluctantly, Burnside withdrew his army to the north bank. On January 25th Lincoln replaced him with Joseph Hooker.

Hooker planned to continue where Burnside had left off. Three things would happen at once, he explained to Lincoln. Federal cavalry under Stoneman would raid behind Lee's left and cut the railroads. General Sedgewick would engage in various diversions at Fredericksburg in order to mislead the rebels into believing that another Burnside-type strategy was planned, while the main army would cross the river's headwaters at several fords. Hooker had 130,000 men, "the finest army on the planet," he called it. Lee could muster less than half as many. Rain delayed the campaign until April 27th when Gen. Stoneman's 6,000 cavalrymen

Shown at left are Federal 32-pounders of Tyler's Connecticut Battery in positions which supported the crossing of Franklin's Grand Division. The ridge beyond the town is Marye's Heights which the Confederates defended during the battle.

Before this house was burned, it served as General Burnside's headquarters for the attack on Fredericksburg. Burnside called his leaders together here and ordered an attack of the heights. They dissuaded him.

Major John "The Gallant" Pelham shelled Federal left with uncanny accuracy using napoleon gun. Lee remarked: "It is glorious to see such courage in one so young." He was killed before age 21.

Shown below is Confederate Sergeant Major Otho S. Lee of Stuart's Horse Artillery. The unit participated in more than one hundred skirmishes in and around the Battle of Fredericksburg.

51

Seen at left reading map is Major Gen. Ambrose E. Burnside and photographer Brady (center in straw hat). The term "sideburns" is a popular corruption of "burnsides," a style of side whiskers worn by, and named for, this general.

Willis' Hill, extending south of Marye's Heights at Fredericksburg, was honeycombed with rifle pits, artillery revetments, and a double line of trenches dug by rebels awaiting Federal attack in Dec., 1862.

Federal Major General Joseph Hooker, "Fighting Joe," was a veteran of the Mexican War. After Chancellorsville he was transferred to the western theater where he distinguished himself at the Battle of Lookout Mountain.

Shown below are ruins in Fredericksburg after Burnside's artillery bombardment. When Confederate sharpshooters fired on Federal pontoniers building floating bridges, Burnside ordered a bombardment of the city.

Shown below is Battery D, 2nd U. S. Artillery, preparing to engage Confederate artillery at Chancellorsville. Rappahannock R., which the battery had just crossed, flows beyond the trees to the rear of the pieces.

In this private railroad car, President and Mrs. Lincoln journeyed to Hooker's headquarters after the latter was appointed head of the Federal Army of the Potomac shortly after the Battle of Fredericksburg.

Shown at right are wounded Federal troops on Marye's Heights. Most are Indians, of whom more than 3,000 served in Union Army. Hospital orderly (kneeling, in hat) is dressing wounds of Indian at left. Note shadowy figure behind tree of man who moved during exposure. All photos had to be posed because of slow plate and shutter speeds.

Federal Major General Oliver O. Howard had lost an arm a year before at the Battle of Fair Oaks. His Eleventh Corps was surprise attacked by Stonewall Jackson's "foot cavalry" at Chancellorsville.

crossed the river and headed south. Federal infantry began moving the same day. On April 30th Sedgewick bridged the river below Fredericksburg to attack Lee's right, and by nightfall Hooker had the bulk of his army across the river.

The next day Federals tramped through thick woods around Chancellorsville, and at noon met Confederates on the Fredericksburg road. Hooker had not expected such early opposition, and doubt as to Lee's location caused him to order a return to Chancellorsville. "From that time" reported a Northerner, "the whole situation was changed. Without striking a blow the army was placed on the defensive."

Taking a bold risk, Lee split his smaller army into three parts. Only enough men to slow the Federals attacking Fredericksburg were left at the town. Others were sent to stall Federals at Chancellorsville. The remainder followed Stonewall Jackson on a fast march to the south behind Hooker. "Throughout the morning of the 2nd of May," remembered a Federal officer,

Shown above are dead artillery horses and destroyed limbers of the Confederate Artillery after the Federal assault on Marye's Heights.

Confederates behind this stone wall stopped Burnside's assault of Marye's Heights in December, 1862. But during Chancellorsville campaign, May, 1863, Federals numbering 22,000 took the stronghold.

This photo of Confederate Lieutenant General Thomas "Stonewall" Jackson was taken two weeks before he was mortally wounded during a skirmish at Chancellorsville. Loss of Jackson to the South was incalculable.

This is a battery of the 1st Connecticut Artillery drilling near Fredericksburg before Chancellorsville. Filled with canister, these 12-pounder napoleon howitzers were as deadly to troops as machine guns.

"attacks were made on different portions of our line from the east to the west—always farther to the west."

Federal General O. O. Howard held Hooker's right flank. "A little after five P.M.," he said, "the steady advance of the enemy began." A Federal aide saw a strange line of battle forming in the dusk through the trees. He galloped out to identify it. "I came to a halt," he said, "peering in the darkness to make sure, when a bullet whistled by me, and then came the rebel yell." In another moment a shocked Howard said that he "could see numbers of our men—not the few stragglers that always fly like the chaff at the first breeze, but scores of them—rushing into the opening, some of them with arms and some without, running or falling."

Disorganized by the pursuit, Confederate attackers milled in the dark woods. Jackson ordered A. P. Hill's fresh division forward to continue the attack, and rode out to scout the Federal position. Federals fired at his group as it moved up the road and Jackson turned to gallop back. Hill's Confederates had no knowledge of anyone but Federals to the front. They opened fire and Stonewall Jackson fell, mortally wounded.

At Fredericksburg, Sedgewick's 22,000 Federals moved at midnight on May 2nd to strike Lee's rear. By dawn Sedgewick reached Fredericksburg, taking the town with little effort. "It was at once felt that a desperate encounter was to follow," recalled one Northerner, "and the recollections of the previous disaster were by no means inspiring." Sedgewick's men began the assault of Marye's Heights shortly before noon. Waiting Confederates opened fire and the 7th Massachusetts lost 150 of its 400 men in the volley. But this time the battle shock was shaken off. Federals stormed the stone wall and pushed Confederate infantrymen for three miles toward Chancellorsville. That night Lee brought substantial forces against Sedgewick who forded back to the north bank.

In the woods around Chancellorsville, with Confederates on all roads, Hooker had found that "it became utterly impossible to maneuver my forces. Accordingly," he added, "when the eight days' rations with which my army started out were exhausted, I retired across the river." Chancellorsville cost the Federal army 17,000.

It cost the Confederates 13,000 and Stonewall Jackson. A Federal officer defined what his death meant to the Confederate army. "He stood head and shoulders above his confréres, and after his death Gen. Lee could not replace him." •

Vicksburg and
Gettysburg

After these two campaigns
the fate of the Confed-
eracy was sealed

IN late 1861, General Ulysses Simpson Grant began an amphibious operation against Columbus, Kentucky, on the Mississippi River. In February, 1862 he captured public attention by seizing Confederate forts on the Cumberland and Tennessee Rivers. There he took 14,000 prisoners at Fort Donelson above Nashville. After stopping a Confederate counter-offensive at Shiloh on the southern Tennessee boundary in April 1862 he shifted to the Confederate bastion Vicksburg, Miss., which controlled the only portion of the Mississippi River still in Confederate hands. It took months of effort. At first he admittedly lacked a plan to take the

Left, Vicksburg, Miss., was the Confederacy's chief river port. Federal capture of the city effectively cut the Confederacy into two parts and prevented transport of supplies from Western Confederate states.

Confederate Major General Martin L. Smith planned and supervised construction of Vicksburg's defenses. Federals called city "a mole hill" because of extensive underground shelters and works.

This naval gun, called "Whistling Dick" because of the peculiar shrill sound its shells made in flight, was a major factor in Confederate defenses at Vicksburg. It shot 18-pound shells and, on May 28, 1863, sunk Federal gunboat "Cincinnati."

Rebel Gen. Pemberton gathered 21,000 men behind Vicksburg's defenses. Grant assaulted the Confederate lines on May 18th and 22nd without result. Both armies dug in as Grant's siege wore rebels down.

The 8th Wisconsin Infantry carried an eagle mascot, "Old Abe" into battle at Vicksburg. Soldiers reported that the bird straightened and flapped its wings; then it flew low over the battlefield.

city, but "There was nothing left to be done but to go forward to a decisive victory," he said.

After digging unprofitable canals during the winter months, Grant marched his men 70 miles down the west riverbank past the city in early 1863. On the night of April 16th a Federal fleet steamed downstream past Vicksburg. Confederates set bonfires and burned houses across the river to silhouette the vessels. "The sight was magnificent, but terrible," said Grant, who watched from a river transport. The gunboats suffered little damage, but one of the transports was burned to the water line.

The fleet ferried Grant's men to the eastern riverbank on April 30th. Abandoning any attempt to obtain supplies from Federal wagon trains in the rear, Grant decided to live off the countryside. He marched on Mississippi's Capital, Jackson. He concentrated his army against smaller Confederate garison forces and destroyed them. Jackson, Miss., fell on May 14th.

Right, after defeating his foes at Champion's Hill near Vicksburg, Grant pursued rebels to Big Black R. and found bridges destroyed. Sherman's men carried pontoon equipment and completed this bridge within twenty-four hours.

Below, new movements by Lee's army led Gen. Hooker to believe that an invasion of the North was impending. These men are engaged in reconnaissance in an attempt to discover the position of Lee's army, which was then advancing toward Gettysburg, Pa.

This stone house on Seminary Ridge, west of Gettysburg, by the road to Chambersburg, served as Lee's headquarters during the early fighting. Tents of Lee's staff members were pitched in the back yard.

Shown above are three outstanding members of Lee's general staff at Gettysburg. Lieutenant Gen. Richard S. Ewell (left), who took command of Stonewall Jackson's corps upon the latter's death, led his troops into Gettysburg during the first day's fighting. Lieut. Gen. James Longstreet (center), considered too confident in his own decisions to be an ideal follower, conducted the rebel attack on the second day. On the third day, Major Gen. James Elwell Brown "Jeb" Stuart (right) led a furious cavalry battle.

Swinging back toward Vicksburg, Grant overwhelmed his foes at Champion's Hill, and again at the Big Black River. In two days he drew his lines around Vicksburg and began starving its defenders. On July 4th, after 47 days of starving and fighting, Vicksburg's defenders surrendered.

By turning back Federal thrusts at Chancellorsville, Virginia, in the spring of 1863, the Southern armies proved brilliant in defense. However, the Confederacy could not survive through a purely defensive policy. A tantalizing rumor was abroad throughout the South that France might intervene on the side of the Confederacy, if a decisive victory could be gained on Northern soil. Moreover, such a victory might convince weary Northerners to give up further efforts to block the Confederacy in her attempt to gain unmolested independence.

On June 3, 1863, Lee began easing his men off to the west, toward the Blue Ridge Mountains, before turning them north. As they marched, Lee studied the prospects of descending on Washington, Baltimore, or Philadelphia. Suspecting something big, Hooker tried to break through the moun-

Federal Major Gen. Gouverneur K. Warren, Chief Engineer at Gettysburg, defended Little Round Top with scattered forces and prevented probable destruction of the Federal line on Cemetery Ridge.

Right, this little house served as Meade's headquarters at Gettysburg. After Rebel charge on the third day, this command post became nearly the center of fighting with artillery shells exploding on all sides of the house.

Left, Major General George G. Meade was commander of all Union forces at Gettysburg. A graduate of West Point, he had extensive engineering experience and helped in prewar harbor works.

63

One of the most daring exploits in the history of warfare was "Pickett's Charge" (below) at Gettysburg. Maj. Gen. George E. Pickett (inset) in a desperate attempt to wrest victory for the South, led 15,000 men up Cemetery Ridge, swept by grape and cannister shot. A small force broke through and captured a battery, but Confederates had entered a death trap and a retreat was ordered. With hat in hand Lee remarked: "It was all my fault—now help me to save that which remains."

tain gaps before Lee, but they were effectively guarded by Southern cavalry. The attempts resulted in a series of cavalry actions beginning at Aldie, Virginia, and extending to the north. By June 25th most of Lee's army was across the Potomac. Three days later Lincoln replaced Hooker with George Meade, a scholarly-looking old regular held in high regard by associates. For once Lee found himself groping. Jeb Stuart's cavalry was off in eastern Pennsylvania raiding under authority of orders which allowed too much to the dashing cavalryman's own discretion. As a consequence, Lee had but a vague knowledge of Federal divisions hurrying up the Potomac's north bank to intercept. "You never saw such a land of plenty," a Confederate wrote his wife on June 28th. "We could live here mighty well for the

next twelve months. Of course, we will have to fight here, and when it comes it will be the biggest on record. We will show the Yankees this time how we can fight."

On the last day of June, Confederates learned of a supply of shoes at Gettysburg, less than ten miles east of Cashtown where they were concentrating. A brigade was quickly put on the road to secure these treasures, but to their surprise, the Confederates found the town occupied by Union soldiers. Upon learning this Lee sent a sizable force into town the next morning. The Confederate advance collided with the advance of Meade's army, Buford's cavalry, at the western outskirts of town. "There was no mistake now," noted a young Northern soldier watching Meade's columns coming up. "While we

Right, this artillery limber was shattered and the horse killed during the second day's fighting at Gettysburg. Limbers such as this were used to carry ammunition, powder, and other artillery equipment.

Each of these Union officers was wounded at Gettysburg. Maj. Gen. Winfield Scott Hancock (seated) organized the Federal defense before Meade's arrival. Standing, left to right, are Major Generals Barlow, Gibbon, and Birney.

Shown above are officers of the 44th New York Infantry. The regiment, whose members averaged 22 years of age, lost 111 men in the desperate struggle for Little Round Top Hill at Gettysburg, Pa.

Right, this photo shows a dead Confederate sharpshooter in the "Devil's Den," a rocky hill 500 yards west of Round Top.

Below right, the "Devil's Den" became a death trap to Longstreet's men who sought shelter there. Many were killed by fragments.

Shown at left is Little Round Top at Gettysburg. Longstreet's troops tried unsuccessfully to fight their way up through these rocks to take the hill, which would enable them to shoot down axis of Federal line.

stood there watching these splendid soldiers file by with their long swinging, 'route-step,' and their muskets glittering in the rays of the rising sun, there came out of the northwest a sullen 'boom! boom! boom!' of three guns, followed almost immediately by a prolonged crackling sound, which, at that distance, reminded one very much of the snapping of a dry brush-heap when you first set it on fire."

Dismounted Federal cavalry fought as infantrymen for the next two hours while both Meade and Lee rushed reinforcements forward. By mid-morning Federal General John Reynolds, one of the Union's rising leaders, had stopped Confederates on the south side of the Cashtown road. While placing new divisions on line Reynolds was struck by a Minie ball, "fired by a sharpshooter hidden in the branches of a tree almost overhead," according to a nearby officer. By mid-afternoon Lee's men worked around to the north flank of the battle position. Confederates of Ewell's corps fought their way into Gettysburg's northern outskirts to drive out the Federal 11th Corps which had received such a set-back at Chancellorsville.

Worried over Stuart's absence with three cavalry brigades, whose roving scouts would have told him the strength of his opposition, Lee refused to allow his commanders to begin a general engagement during the afternoon before the bulk of his army arrived. That night Meade arrived at the scene to find that General Hancock had placed Federal units on the strongest natural position, the low ridge stretching southeast of town. Its name was Cemetery Ridge from the cemetery located there, and its south end was terminated by a hill—Little Round Top.

Opposite Cemetery Ridge to the west was a parallel rise called Seminary Ridge from the school atop it. Lee's Confederates deployed there during the night and studied the mile of open fields and orchards separating the two armies. Determined to assault Meade as he found him, Lee placed his troops in attack positions during the sultry night of July 1st. Time was critical. He must strike before more

Shown at right is a dead Confederate soldier behind rocks which he piled up to protect himself. He is Private Andrew J. Hoge of the 4th Virginia Infantry and was killed July 3 at the age of 18.

At Gettysburg the Federal army lost 3,063 killed, 14,492 wounded, and 5,435 missing. Loss to Confederates was 3,903 killed, 18,735 wounded and 5,425 missing. Loss to both armies totalled 51,053.

Right, these Union troops were killed during the fighting at Gettysburg. Lincoln, in his famous Gettysburg Address, declared, "We here highly resolve that these dead shall not have died in vain."

enemy troops arrived on the field. Longstreet, on the Confederate right, was to lead the attack the next day. Unfortunately, his troops were still marching in from bivouacs as far as 24 miles away during the morning and early afternoon. The attack began at 5 p. m., aimed up the Emittsburg road, a maneuver which would cut off Little Round Top. The hill's possession would allow Confederates to shoot down along the axis of the Federal line.

Federal engineer Warren, scouting Little Round Top in late afternoon, was dismayed to find it unguarded. Gathering scattered troops together, he led them on the run to block Confederates already climbing its rocky slopes. By dusk Longstreet's attack had been effectively stalled by General Sickle's stubborn resistance in a peach orchard and wheat field before Cemetery Ridge, and the Confederates found the Federal main line unbroken when they stopped their attack after dark. On July 3rd Lee made a last desperate

attempt. Led by General George Pickett, 15,000 Confederates poured across the open valley, headed toward the center of the Federal line. A few reached the fence atop Cemetery Ridge, a point which came to be known as the "high water mark of the Confederacy." Then they were thrown back by Federal troops attacking on all sides, and riddled Confederate lines straggled back across the fields. A shocked Lee rode out to meet the remnants, and attempted to console them. "It's all my fault!" he told them. "It's all my fault!"

Jeb Stuart rode in during the battle, exuberant over the capture of 200 Federal supply wagons, but he was too late. The large-scale cavalry battle east of the main battle line which he generated during the afternoon of July 3rd was furious but it accomplished nothing. On July 4th neither army moved. That night Lee's men loaded wounded on a wagon train 17 miles long and turned south toward the Potomac. •

After the fighting, Little Round Top was strewn with Union and Confederate dead. The Southerners were driven off the hill three times in ferocious hand-to-hand fighting before they succumbed.

Shown at left is the Trostle's House, headquarters of Federal Gen. Sickles. Well in advance of Union lines, it was scene of bloody carnage as Rebels attacked and drove the men back to the main line.

Chickamauga and Chattanooga

Capture of Chattanooga would split Confederacy's heartland.

Photo below is of the Battle of Shiloh (Pittsburg Landing) in Southern Tennessee, where these Federal heavy artillery pieces stopped the Confederates. In this battle both sides lost more than 10,000 men.

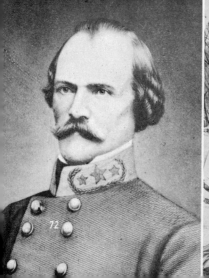

IN the summer of 1862, the Union army, west of the Appalachians, pushed deep into Mississippi. But by the middle of September the Southerners had shifted eastward from the Federal front to eastern Tennessee, and pushed north again into Kentucky, threatening Louisville on the Ohio River. The maneuver came close to neutralizing the hard-earned Federal victories at Fort Donelson, Shiloh and Corinth. Except for Nashville, Central Tennessee was again under Confederate control. Rebel General Braxton Bragg became worried about supply lines and after fighting the Federal army at Perryville, Kentucky, he withdrew southward

Right, Federal Major General Gordon Granger served with special distinction at Chickamauga, when he took his three brigades to relieve General Thomas. They arrived at the critical moment to stop a fresh charge of Confederates. Shown above Granger is the Battlefield of Lee and Gordon's Mills, on the west branch of Chickamauga Creek. Here, Gen. Rosecrans wrestled Bragg from Tennessee.

On opposite page at extreme left is Confederate General Albert Sidney Johnston, who was killed during the first day's fighting at Shiloh. To his right is an on-the-spot drawing which depicts Federal General W. B. Hazen's 19th Brigade charging at Shiloh. The thin lines of charging troops shown here were used extensively during the war's first battles, but repeating rifles rendered them obsolete.

into Tennessee. He established a line across the state a few miles southeast of Nashville, and held it for nearly a year while Grant's army attacked Vicksburg.

Opposing Bragg was Major-General William S. Rosecrans, who had one objective—Chattanooga, Tennessee, a town of less than ten thousand, but the weakest point of the rail network over the central south. Located in rugged Appalachian country, the town's single railroad connected substantial rail systems to both sides of the mountains. Rosecrans realized that capture of Chattanooga would effectively

General Gordon Granger waited here at the John Ross house, in the Rossville Gap overlooking Chattanooga. Taking his troops forward, he saved Federal army of General Thomas from destruction.

Below is shown the Louisville and Nashville R.R. bridge across the Cumberland River at Nashville. These heavy gates at both ends prevented raiders from entering; riflemen guarded from towers.

Below, Federal Major General Thomas, the "Rock of Chickamauga," succeeded to the command of Rosecrans' army at Chattanooga. A native of Virginia, Thomas was a lieutenant colonel at the start of war.

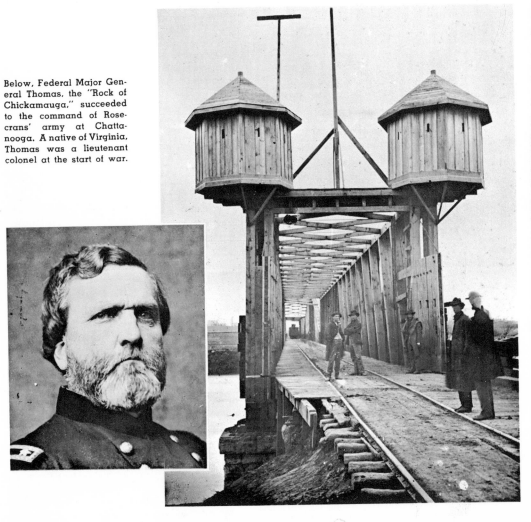

split the heartland of the South. On December 31, 1862, the forces of Rosecrans engaged those of Bragg in the flat plain outside Murfreesboro, Tennessee, and fought the battle of Stone's River. Both generals had the same plan—to attack the enemy's left. Stopped the first day, Confederates charged forward the next into the fire of fifty cannon concealed at their flank. These batteries halted further action and both armies picked up a fourth of their men who had fallen during the battle.

Bragg withdrew slowly toward Chattanooga and held Rosecrans at bay for the next half year. After feinting against the north side of the Confederate line in late summer, Rosecrans sent his long columns around the south end. To protect the Confederate rear, Bragg dropped back into Chattanooga, and then into northern Georgia. Rosecrans hurried one column into Chattanooga. Another was sent across the mountains to strike below the city and a third column was dispatched twenty miles further to the south to block fleeing Confederates. Bragg's columns suddenly drew back near Chickamauga, Ga., a few miles from Chattanooga, with the aim of

These "contraband" (freed) slaves are repairing the railroad near Murfreesboro, Tennessee, after the battle of Stone's River. After emancipation the Federal army employed Negroes and paid them wages.

Right, this view of Federal Fort Sanders (on horizon) was taken across the Holston River near Knoxville. Longstreet attempted to take Fort Sanders, lost 1,000 men, and abandoned the campaign of Knoxville.

75

Shown above is a view of
the rebuilt Falling Water
Bridge with Federal block-
house (foreground) guard-
ing it. The U. S. Army stationed large forces around
all key points on its supply
lines near Chattanooga.

Left, Federal army engi-
neers built this trestle
bridge on the Chattanooga
and Nashville R.R. after
it was destroyed by the
retreating Confederates.
The bridge was 116 feet
high and 780 feet in length.

destroying the center Federal column. Federal commanders drew back exposed forces and felled trees across roads to delay Gen. Bragg's troops. The Confederate line stretched along the south bank of a creek named by Indians Chickamauga, "river of death." The Federal line was built on the north bank. Crossing to the wooded north bank, Bragg opened the battle of Chickamauga with an attack on September 18, 1863. "The enemy are in plain view along the road covering our entire front," wrote a waiting Federal soldier. "You can see them, as with cap visors drawn well down over their eyes, the gun at the charge, with short, shrill shouts they come."

Above right, this trestle bridge at Bridgeport, Ala., was begun by Sheridan's men on July 31, 1863. Using timber from nearby woods, barns and houses, it was completed and men began moving across on Sept. 2.

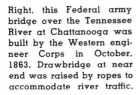

Right, this Federal army bridge over the Tennessee River at Chattanooga was built by the Western engineer Corps in October, 1863. Drawbridge at near end was raised by ropes to accommodate river traffic.

The Nashville and Northwestern Railroad was a 70-mile line connecting Tennessee's Capital with Johnsonville on the Tennessee River. The railroad supplied Federal armies during Battle of Chattanooga.

Below left, Major General Braxton Bragg was commander of Confederates at Shiloh as well as Chickamauga and Chattanooga. Ill tempered and often stubborn, Bragg was not popular with his subordinates. To his right is shown the Federal steamer Bridgeport, being unloaded at Chattanooga on the Tennessee River.

This Federal steamer is being hauled through the "Suck," a narrow gorge through Raccoon Mountain west of Chattanooga, where strong current required that windlasses be used to pull steamers upstream.

Confederate General Longstreet's corps arrived during the battle, his soldiers rushed 843 miles from Lee's Army of Northern Virginia by rail. Troops jumped from slowing box cars and ran at a dogtrot toward the battle.

On the second day of battle, a Federal commander, puzzled by a poorly-worded order, pulled his unit out of the Federal line to shift position. Longstreet's men, advancing in a general assault, struck this hole by accident and the Federal line broke. Federal General George Thomas earned the title of "the Rock of Chickamauga" by rallying his men on a spur of Missionary Ridge where they slowed ad-

vancing Confederates. Gordon Granger's troops rushed to reinforce the bulwark and Rosecrans' army was saved as it gathered in Chattanooga, two miles behind Missionary Ridge. Over 35,000 soldiers, North and South, were casualties, the Southerners losing more in victory than the Northerners in defeat.

While Rosecrans built a hasty defense line around Chattanooga, Bragg's troops moved in close to the city, fortifying Missionary Ridge and blocking eastern approaches and Lookout Mountain, overlooking the city from the southwest. Bragg placed artillery on Lookout Mountain to harass traffic on the Tennessee River,

which curved behind the city from the mountain to the north end of Missionary Ridge. Before long, starving Federal soldiers at Chattanooga began following supply wagons to glean grains of corn from the mud, while Federal engineers built steamboats for the "cracker line," which brought supplies of hardtack from north Alabama. General Sherman was summoned from Memphis with a relief column, Grant was put in charge of all Federal forces between the Alleghanies and the Mississippi, and Rosecrans was displaced by Thomas.

On November 22nd, Grant learned that the Confederates were shifting supplies to the rear, and an exploratory attack was

Above, Pulpit Rock at the peak of Lookout Mountain overlooked Federal-held Chattanooga. Joseph Hooker's men seized these heights from the Confederates who were outnumbered six to one in the "Battle Above the Clouds."

These artillery crewmen, here relaxing after Battle of Chattanooga, manned a battery which kept encircling Rebels away from Tennessee R. so rafts of firewood could be floated to the beleaguered garrison.

This photo was made a few weeks after the Battle of Chattanooga. The Federal army parked these captured Confederate napoleon 12-pounders near Gen. Thomas' headquarters. Rebels lost 52 cannon.

made the next day toward Missionary Ridge to determine whether Bragg still held in force. "Flags were flying; the quick earnest steps of thousands beat equal time," remembered a Northerner.

O. O. Howard of Chancellorsville and Gettysburg, had just arrived from the East. He watched the Federal marchers gain their limited objectives with little effort. The next day Hooker drove the Confederate detachment off fog-shrouded Lookout Mountain while thousands of Federal soldiers watching from Chattanooga cheered. On November 25th Grant sent Sherman against the north end of Missionary Ridge and Hooker against its south end. As fighting slowed in late after-

noon, Grant ordered seizure of the Confederate rifle pits at the foot of the ridge.

Federal infantry swept over the Confederate rifle pits, but to their commander's consternation, did not stop. As they climbed after fleeing Confederates, Grant turned angrily to General Thomas—"Who ordered those men up the ridge?"

"I don't know; I did not." Thomas turned to Granger, "Did you order them up?" Granger said that he didn't. Grant muttered darkly that it had better turn out all right or someone would suffer. A few minutes later the Confederate line atop the ridge broke in six places and Confederates streamed south in a rout toward Dalton, Georgia. •

Confederates, captured on Missionary Ridge, await shipment. U. S. War Secretary Stanton reported that 26,436 Southern soldiers died in Northern prisons and 22,576 Union troops died in Confederate prisons.

This house in Chattanooga was headquarters of General Thomas. Here, on the evening of October 23, 1863, Grant conferred with Thomas to plan for supply buildup permitting Federal army to break out of city.

MERRIMAC

MONITOR

Naval Warfare

The Federal blockade strangled Southern ocean commerce.

ALTHOUGH the Federal Navy expanded to include 569 steam vessels and 58 ironclads with revolving turrets by the end of the war, it began modestly with only 42 vessels and 6,700 sailors. At the conclusion of hostilities, in April, 1865, the Navy mustered over 51,000 men. With few exceptions the Federal Navy performed with little fanfare, but with telling effectiveness.

Of most importance in wearing down the Confederacy's power to resist was the blockade begun on April 19, 1861, after the secession of South Carolina, Georgia and the Gulf states. As successive states joined the Confederacy, a thin line of Federal ships drew cordons across Southern harbor entrances. Because of its effectiveness in strangling Southern ocean commerce, the blockade was dubbed "Scott's Anaconda" in reference to the Army General-in-Chief, Winfield Scott.

The only practical means available to the Confederates to circumvent the blockade was through the use of blockade runners. The fastest vessels in the European merchant services were loaded with supplies needed by the Confederacy, and, on dark nights, the ships slipped through the Federal cordon. British commercial firms invested heavily in the venture since cotton worth eight cents a pound in the South was worth sixty in England. When blockade running was at its height in 1863, a Confederate officer estimated that Southern ports received a blockade runner a day. A Northerner reported "Officers of rank in the Royal navy under assumed names, officers of the Confederate navy who had but just resigned from the United States Navy, and adventurous spirits from all quarters flocked to this new and profitable, though hazardous, occupation. The Con-

Throughout the entire war it was more difficult to recruit seamen than soldiers and bounties were offered enlistees by the war's end. Many sailors were drawn from the ranks of the United States Merchant Marine.

At left is the U.S.S. "Pensacola" at Alexandria, Va., 1861. This sloop-of-war combined steam power with sails and was commissioned less than 5 years before the war together with the "Hartford," Farragut's flagship.

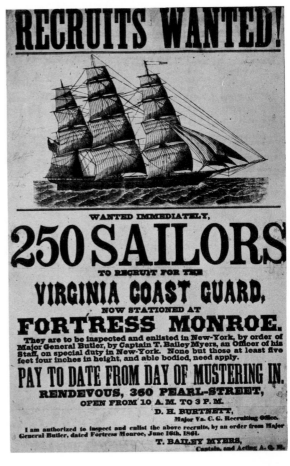

RECRUITS WANTED!

WANTED IMMEDIATELY,

250 SAILORS

TO RECRUIT FOR THE

VIRGINIA COAST GUARD,

NOW STATIONED AT

FORTRESS MONROE.

They are to be inspected and enlisted in New-York, by order of Major General Butler, by Captain T. Bailey Myers, an Officer of his Staff, on special duty in New-York. None but those at least five feet four inches in height, and able bodied, need apply.

PAY TO DATE FROM DAY OF MUSTERING IN.

RENDEVOUS, 360 PEARL-STREET,

OPEN FROM 10 A. M. TO 3 P. M.

D. H. BURTNETT,
Major Va. C. G. Recruiting Office.

I am authorized to inspect and enlist the above recruits, by an order from Major General Butler, dated Fortress Monroe, June 16th, 1861.

T. BAILEY MYERS,
Captain, and Acting A. Q. M.

Confederate ram "Stonewall" was built in France and launched in January, 1865. She could turn on her center in 90 seconds, compared with 15 minutes for sailing vessels, and carried Armstrong guns.

federate government also embarked in the business, procuring swift steamers from English builders, officered with Confederate naval officers, and sailing under the British ensign."

"Some of these blockade-runners were very successful," said a Charleston citizen. "I knew of one which had run the gauntlet no less than nineteen times. When a vessel had once run the blockade it was considered to have paid for itself, and every subsequent trip was consequently clear gain."

It was estimated that the blockade was thwarted 8,000 times. The U. S. Navy captured or destroyed 1,504 blockade runners. The Southern navy began even more modestly than the Northern. Although 322 U. S. Naval officers resigned and joined the Confederacy, there were no ships upon which to build a Southern navy. To overcome this, a dozen privateers were authorized and given letters of marque by the Confederate government.

A captured Federal ship captain de-

Photograph above shows the deck of the steamer "Hudson," first blockade runner captured by U. S. Navy.

Painting at right depicts Confederate blockade runners in port at St. George, Bermuda. That island, as well as the Bahamas, were sanctuaries for these fast steamers which slipped into Southern ports at night.

Below, early experimental ironclad, U.S.S. "Galena," was a small corvette with her sides plated with three inches of iron armor. The ship was damaged beyond repair in an attack on Ft. Darling on May 15, 1862.

scribed the tactics of one such privateer in a Charleston paper. "At 8:30 the privateer tacked and stood N. W., at the same time setting a French ensign, and from the fact of her having French-cut hempen sails we supposed she was a French merchant brig. At 9 o'clock, to our surprise, she fired a shot across our bows and hove to. Just before the boat came alongside the French flag was hauled down and the Confederate flag run up. In about two minutes afterwards the armed crew was on our deck."

Eighteen cruisers were purchased abroad by the Confederacy. These wreaked such havoc with Northern commerce on the open seas that it was not until World War One that the merchant fleet recovered as much as a third of the tonnage it had in 1860.

Most famous of Southern raiding cruisers was the *Alabama,* built by an English firm. Upon completion in mid-1862, she sailed from England as an unarmed vessel to a rendezvous in the Azores accompanied by a transport ship which carried her guns and war materiel.

The *Alabama's* 300-horsepower engines yielded a top speed of 15 knots, and she carried condensers to provide fresh water from the ocean, thus permitting long periods at sea. Other supplies were taken from captured vessels.

Her captain, Raphael Semmes, was a

Drawing on opposite page depicts battle, off France, between the Confederacy's most famous raider, the C.S.S. "Alabama" (right) and the U.S.S. "Kearsarge," June 19, 1864. The battle lasted more than an hour with the result that the "Alabama" went to the bottom of the English Channel. Her commander, Rear Admiral Raphael Semmes (left) subsequently served as Brigadier of Rebel army.

Below, on March 9, 1862, the Civil War's most significant naval battle took place at Hampton Roads between the U.S.S. "Monitor" and the C.S.S. "Virginia," popularly called the "Merrimac." Confederate Captain Franklin Buchanan (left inset) took the untried 5-knot "Merrimac" into battle against the Federal blockading squadron off Norfolk. Her success panicked Washington for fear of a naval bombardment. The next day the "Monitor," commanded by Lt. J. L. Worden (right inset) fought the "Merrimac" to a draw for two hours. Both ships withdrew and the "Merrimac" was subsequently scuttled to prevent its capture by the Federal Navy.

Photo at left, made after the famous battle, shows the dents in the "Monitor's" turret, which indicate the strength of her armor. She was struck 22 times with negligible damage scoring 42 hits on "Merrimac."

Federal gunboat "Commodore Perry," a converted ferry, captured flagship of guarding Confederate naval forces off Roanoke Island, N. C., in February, 1862. During summer she steamed up Roanoke R. and seized another boat.

former lawyer and veteran U. S. Naval officer. Under his command, the *Alabama* captured 66 vessels and burned 52. She attacked Northern shipping from New England to South America and Europe. She raided the Caribbean, Gulf of Mexico, central Atlantic, Indian Ocean, East Indies, Madagascar, and the Azores.

In June, 1864, the Federal "screw-sloop" *Kearsarge* arrived off Cherbourg, France, to find the *Alabama* in the harbor. As soon as the *Kearsarge* came into the harbor, Captain Semmes sent for his executive officer and abruptly said to him "Kell, I am going to fight the *Kearsarge*. What do you think of it?"

Hoping to battle at long range with solid shot, Semmes was surprised to find his opponent closing uncomfortably during the Sunday duel. This strategy was the *Alabama's* undoing for "the *Kearsarge* was really in the fullest sense of the word a man-of-war," according to a Confederate naval officer, "staunch and well-built, the

Alabama was made for flight and speed and was much more lightly constructed."

The *Kearsarge* was successful in firing 11-inch high-explosive shells through her opponent's waterline, and while 15,000 spectators on Cherbourg's cliffs watched, the *Alabama* sank stern first.

Seeking continually to find a type of ship to sink blockading Federal squadrons, the Confederates raised the scuttled U.S.S. *Merrimac* from Norfolk waters, refitted her, and clad her sides in iron. On her trial run she steamed out to engage wooden Federal vessels in Hampton Roads on March 8, 1862.

A Federal sailor aboard the U.S.S. *Congress* described the next few minutes. "She fired a gun at us. It went clean through the ship and killed nobody. The next one was a shell. It came in at a porthole, killed six men, and exploded and killed nine more. The next one killed ten. Then she went down to the *Cumberland*." This Federal ship fought until "her gun-deck was under

Shown above are crewmen of the Federal gunboat "Mendota." A marine is playing checkers with a sailor before the capstan upon which a young powder monkey leans. "Mendota" mounted two 200-pounder guns.

Photo below is of the 32-pounder gun on Confederate gunboat "Teaser," a converted river tug. She took part in the Battle of Hampton Roads. On July 4, "Teaser" was sunk in engagement on James River.

Confederate cannoneers are engaged in gun drill in Warrington, Pensacola Bay, Florida. Rebels never succeeded in seizing nearby Fort Pickens on Sta. Rosa Is. guarding approaches to Pensacola.

water," the sailor said, "but her shot had no more effect than peas." The *Merrimac* sank the *Cumberland* in seven fathoms of water and ran three more Federal warships aground. She was opposed in battle the next day by the Federal "tin can on a shingle" *Monitor*. The *Merrimac* limped back to Norfolk and shortly thereafter suffered an inglorious demise by scuttling when Confederates evacuated the city and were unable to take the ship into shallow river waters.

Confederate states tried to provide adequate seacoast artillery for their harbors, but that method of defense was already outmoded. Federal bombarding squadrons massed unmolested off such harbor forts and reduced them one by one.

When surrender was not obtained by naval bombardment, Federal troops were landed on the beaches behind Confederate forts where they began methodical siege operations to reduce the bastions from poorly-defended landward sides. The Cape Hatteras area of sand banks off North Carolina received first Federal priority since the many islands and sounds were difficult to blockade effectively.

In August, 1861, the U. S. Navy, under Flag Officer Silas Stringham, landed Benjamin Butler's troops on Hatteras Island while naval gunfire bombarded one of two forts guarding Hatteras Inlet into surrender. By the next day the other fort ran up the white flag. It didn't amount to much of a victory, according to Admiral Porter, since Federal ships brought 158 guns to bear against 25, but it was a satisfying triumph only a month after the Federal disaster at Bull Run.

In the fall of 1861, a Federal amphibious task force, sailing under secret orders, secured an operating base at Port Royal, South Carolina, below Charleston. After shelling Confederates out of guarding forts, the ships put Federal army forces ashore to garrison the Hilton Head area.

Ship Island, in the Gulf of Mexico, off Biloxi, Mississippi, was seized in September as an advanced base for Farragut's operations against New Orleans, and for use as a supply point for blockading squadrons along the Gulf coast.

Early in 1862, General Ambrose Burnside moved an amphibious force against Roanoke Island in the protected shallow sounds behind Nag's Head, North Carolina. His troops were landed on February 7th and fought their way through salt marshes and pine woods across the island to the

Below is a rare photo of U.S. Navy's most famous Civil War figure, Adm. David G. Farragut. He seized New Orleans and later steamed into Mobile Bay saying, "Damn the torpedoes, full speed ahead."

This young Federal "powder monkey" was aboard U.S.S. "New Hampshire" on the blockading fleet of Charleston, S. C. The 100-pounder Parrott gun behind him could shell targets four miles away.

Fort Pulaski surrendered after two days' bombardment by 36 rifled cannon and mortars. Major General David Hunter (inset), who led seizure, later became the first Federal General to use Negro troops.

The guns of this Confederate water battery at Fort Johnson, Charleston S. C., kept the Federal fleet 2 miles offshore.

Fort Sumter and Charleston remained a challenge to Federal military operations throughout the war, and a major effort was directed against them. Federal batteries were set up in coastal swamps and dunes.

These 100-pounder Parrott rifles in Federal Fort Putnam dropped 80,000 shells into Charleston and Fort Sumter. However the Confederates held until fort was nearly cut off from inland communications.

main Confederate fortifications. The next day the Confederate garrison surrendered 2,700 prisoners and thirty artillery pieces, and the island became a staging base for movement against New Berne and Beaufort, North Carolina. By the next month both cities were in Federal hands.

The principal Confederate port south of Charleston, Savannah, Georgia, was out of reach. The city was located up the Savannah River whose mouth was protected by Fort Pulaski. However, Confederate artillerymen there counted over sixty Federal vessels on the horizon one spring morning in 1862, and soon found themselves faced with a Federal army which came ashore and began digging its way around them.

Federal seige guns soon demonstrated again the effect of heavy artillery against

mortared walls, and the battered defenders ran up the surrender flag before General David Hunter's infantry had a chance to storm the works.

Most coveted of all Southern ports, however, was Charleston, South Carolina. The rebellion had started there, and the recapture of Fort Sumter had become a consuming mission for Federal effort all out of proportion to its real military value.

In early 1863, the Federal Secretary of Navy authorized a naval operation against it. On April 7th nine ironclads confidently steamed up to Fort Sumter to demand its surrender but when the ironclads got within 600 yards, the Confederates in Sumter, and supporting batteries at Fort Moultrie and Cumming's Point, opened such an intense fire that the Federal ships swung

Photo below is of Federal mortar crews in action near Fort Sumter. An observer on the parapet watches the explosion of each shot and calls instruction to crew for adjustment of range and angle to the target.

This Confederate 10-inch Columbiad, in Charleston's South Battery, was a smoothbore gun which could shell a target over 3 miles away. One such gun fired 600-pound shells at Federal positions.

Scene below is inside Confederate-held Fort Sumter. These 15-inch Columbiads fired 428-pound shells. Rebels evacuated Fort on the night of February 17, 1865, when Charleston was abandoned.

This is the turret of the Federal monitor, U.S.S. "Catskill." On July 10, 1863, the "Catskill" led a naval attack against Fort Sumter. She fired 128 rounds and received 60 hits, many piercing her armor.

This rare action photo by George S. Cook shows shell exploding in Fort Sumter on September 8, 1863. Confederate Commander Major Stephen Elliot (right) refused Federal surrender demand of day before.

Fort Sumter's defenders found that sand was better fortification than granite. Stone and masonry were reduced to rubble while displaced sand was shoveled back into place.

Federal boat parties attempted to take Fort Sumter on the night of September 7, 1863, but were repulsed. Another unsuccessful assault was attempted over this beach on the following evening.

Although Fort Sumter's 40-foot cement and brick walls were battered, her defenders shoveled the debris back into place and returned shell for shell. Her guns scored 190 hits on ironclads during battle.

At left is shown the Confederate arsenal at Charleston, S. C. Manufacture of arms and ammunition lagged in the Confederacy and captured arms were imitated. Weapons were improvised or imported.

This 20-inch Lincoln Gun, at Fort Monroe, was the largest made during the war. The 57-ton Federal weapon fired a half-ton projectile over 4½ miles; it was fired but 4 times during war.

The muzzle was shot away on this Confederate Columbiad at Fort Fisher, N. C. The largest naval task force of the war bombarded Fisher in December, 1864. Fort was taken by Federal army troops.

Charleston received severe shelling by Federal artillery batteries beginning in August, 1863. Ruins of Secession Hall are to the right of Circular Church, seen here with scaffolding around its tower.

around to head seaward. Five ironclads were disabled in the forty-five minute exchange.

Shortly a 10,000-man Federal army force landed on beaches south of Charleston and began preparations to shell Fort Sumter into surrender. Batteries were emplaced in the swamplands. "About 450 projectiles struck the fort daily," reported the Federal commander, "everyone of which inflicted an incurable wound. Large masses of the brick walls and parapets were rapidly loosened and thrown down. The bulk of our fire was directed against the gorge and southeast face, which presented themselves diagonally to us. They were soon pierced through and through."

But defenders rebuilt earth walls. "From having been a desolate ruin," wrote a Confederate engineer, "Fort Sumter under fire was transformed within a year into a powerful earth-work, impregnable to assault, and even supporting the other works at the entrance of Charleston harbor with six guns of the heaviest caliber."

A Confederate sand fort, Fort Wagner, received nearly 125,000 pounds of Federal shells without significant damage, and had to be taken by assaulting Federal infantry.

Only when Sherman's Federal army turned north from Savannah in early 1865, after its march through Georgia, and threatened to isolate the Charleston area were Fort Sumter and Charleston evacuated. More significant was the capture of Fort Fisher, which guarded Wilmington, N. C. It surrendered on Jan. 15, 1865. Wilmington, the last Southern port of consequence, fell a month later. The blockade could no longer be penetrated. •

Wilderness and Shenandoah Campaigns

The forces of Grant were pitted against those of Lee, while the Federal Capital was threatened.

ON March 9, 1864, Ulysses Simpson Grant was promoted to the rank of lieutenant general and was placed in supreme command of all Federal armies. "You are vigilant and self-reliant," Lincoln wrote, "and pleased with this, I wish not to obtrude any constraints or restraints upon you. If there is anything wanting which is within my power to give, do not fail to let me know it."

By spring Grant was ready to begin the coordinated movements of Federal armies which would segment the Confederacy and allow final destruction of its shrinking forces. While Sherman marched from Chattanooga into Georgia to destroy the

In March, 1864, Lieutenant Gen. Ulysses S. Grant was appointed General-in-Chief of the Union Army.

Grant's first supply base in his Virginia campaign was here at Belle Plain, which was located at the confluence of Potomac Creek with the Potomac R.

Right, this pencil drawing, made by A. R. Waud, depicts wounded soldiers being carried by stretcher bearers from the burning woods of the Wilderness.

Shown at left is Benham's wharf at Belle Plain Landing, Virginia. This wharf was built by the Federal Engineer Corps under Gen. H. W. Benham in May.

only effective Confederate force in the deep South, Grant launched Meade's Army of the Potomac against Lee in Virginia. Leaving Washington, Grant took the field with Meade's forces. The initial obstacles facing Meade's army were the streams above Fredericksburg and the thickets of second-growth timber around Chancellorsville known as the Wilderness. .

Grant began moving the Federal army across the streams and into the Wilderness on the night of May 2nd. By the 4th it was across in force. Lee was pleased, for this was the only place where he might reduce the odds against him. The resulting Battle of the Wilderness took place, according to

a Federal artilleryman, "on a line approximately four miles long by about 90,000 troops on our side and 65,000 on theirs, and there was no open ground anywhere with enough for a division to deploy on."

By the afternoon of May 5th two separate battles were under way. The next day Federals broke the Confederate right, and Lee rallied his line only when Longstreet's men hurried in from Gordonsville, 30 miles away. As his columns converged in dense woods, Longstreet was wounded by his own soldiers, and the counterattack bogged down. The next day burning underbrush threatened the wounded between the armies, and fighting flared sporadically.

This dead Southern lad was found near a farm-house at Spotsylvania. He bandaged his leg with a shirt, but bled to death from a shoulder wound.

Federal Major General John Sedge-wick was killed at Spotsylvania by a Confederate sharpshooter on May 9.

Federal Major Gen. Francis G. Barlow led a charge which resulted in capture of 4,000 Rebels and 20 cannon.

Confederates astride the roads to the west and south caused Grant no concern. "Make all preparations during the day for a night march to take position at Spotsylvania Court House," he instructed Meade at dawn on May 7th.

When Lee learned of the Federal movement toward Spotsylvania some ten miles to the southeast, he pushed Longstreet's corps toward the vicinity. As both armies hurried toward Spotsylvania, the battle opened between advance groups. Determined opponents dug in, and Confederates fought off charge after charge, but soon found their line bent back severely, the apex forming an exposed salient into which

Right, Gen. Sedgewick's body was taken to Spotsylvania, where burial detail has paused for rest.

Left, these Union soldiers, wounded in the Wilderness campaign, are resting at Fredericksburg. More than 24,000 on both sides were wounded in Wilderness.

Drawing at left shows Barlow's charge at Cold Harbor, which took place on June 3, 1864. Drawing, by A. R. Waud, appeared in Harper's magazine, June 25.

101

These 50th New York Engineers are building a road along south bank of North Anna R. Existing roads could not accommodate men and supplies.

These Federal troops, wounded during the Wilderness campaign, are being cared for by the nurses of the Sanitary Commission at Fredericksburg, Va.

Federals on both sides could fire. Heavy rain slowed fighting, and on May 19th, Grant slipped half his army southeast again, forcing Lee to come along as a barrier before Richmond.

Lee withdrew across the next major obstacle, the North Anna River, where he built an enviable defense on high ground shaped like a spearhead, with its tip resting on the south bank. Unaware of its potential, pursuing Federal divisions streamed across, unwittingly splitting Grant's army on this natural spear point. At the critical moment, when Lee was poised to mass against either segment, illness overcame him and alerted Federals

This photo, taken on May 12, 1864, shows Federal soldiers, killed during the Wilderness and Spotsylvania campaigns, being carried on stretchers to their places of burial.

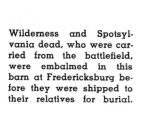

Casualties, numbering 50,-000 during the Wilderness campaign, were so great that there was little time to bury fallen soldiers. There were nearly 18,000 casualties in the woodlands alone.

Wilderness and Spotsylvania dead, who were carried from the battlefield, were embalmed in this barn at Fredericksburg before they were shipped to their relatives for burial.

shifted back to the north bank. Grant pointed Meade downstream to maneuver the Confederates out of position again by threatening Richmond. Lee followed. On June 3rd Grant attacked at Cold Harbor, a crossroads 10 miles east of Richmond. The Confederates had been drawn out of the protecting woodlands where superior Federal numbers could overwhelm them. A storm of lead Minie balls and cannister shot from Confederate small arms and artillery decimated Federals charging across Cold Harbor's open ground. An estimated 13,000 Federals were shot down at Second Cold Harbor, most of them within eight minutes. "I have always regretted that the last assault was ever made," reflected Grant solemnly, "no advantage whatever was gained to compensate for the heavy loss we sustained." Some 54,000 Federal soldiers had been taken out of action.

Grant built his lines before Richmond and Petersburg, while Lee sent a diversion from the Shenandoah Valley to threaten Washington. The diversion was led by Jubal Early, a man reminiscent of the adventurous Stonewall Jackson. Always daring, and unperturbed by setbacks on the battlefield, Early crossed the Potomac on July 4, 1864, under orders to "threaten Washington." Angry at Federal David Hunter's depredations in north Virginia,

Early exacted revenge as he moved. Frederick, Maryland, was ransomed for $200,000 on threat of burning. Federals at Martinsburg and the Monocacy River were brushed aside, and after two dusty days of marching, which covered 60 miles, Early approached lightly-defended Fort Stevens at Washington's western outskirts. Even as he scouted it, however, Federal defense forces rushed to fill the earthworks before him, and Early found that further attack was useless. He eluded pursuit and returned to Virginia.

Of concern to Federal commanders in northern Virginia was Mosby's band of regularly enlisted Confederate horsemen

The embalming surgeon is treating the body of a Union soldier killed in the Wilderness. The arrangements were usually made by the companions of fallen soldiers.

Rebel leader of Shenandoah struggle was resourceful, aggressive Maj. Gen. Jubal Early. Halted only by Sheridan's superior forces, Lee playfully called him "my bad old man."

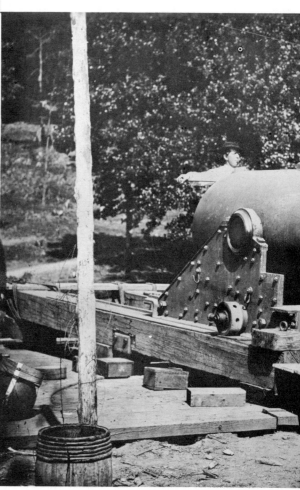

Above, this 15-inch Rodman smoothbore was emplaced near Washington for Capital's defense.

Huge Rodman guns such as this one were mounted along the banks of the Potomac River in order to forestall naval attacks upon the National Capital by Confederate gunboats.

Early's men approached Washington and came within sight of the unfinished U. S. Capitol (above).

Sentries guarded this chain bridge across the Potomac near Washington to prevent surprise attack.

Shown below is a six-pounder rifled cannon at the Washington, D. C., arsenal, which stocked a large inventory of artillery of various types.

Above right, Company L, 2nd New York Artillery is shown here drilling in Fort Smith near Washington. Less than 10,000 men, mostly recruits, manned Washington's defenses when Jubal Early first attacked.

Guerrilla raids in northern Virginia by Rebel John Mosby necessitated the building of these defensive stockades. They were placed across principal streets, and gates were guarded by sentries.

who operated as Partisan Rangers, a status authorized by Confederate law in April 1862. John Mosby, a young Virginia lawyer, recruited soldiers on leave, farmhands, and occasionally a Federal deserter. Supplied by friendly farmers, Mosby took orders from Lee's cavalry chief. His activities chiefly comprised train wrecking, burning Federal supply wagons and capturing Federals for intelligence purposes. Only when the Shenandoah was devastated by Sheridan and the Blue Ridge Mountains were overrun did "Mosby's Confederacy" lose its power to draw Federal regiments away from front lines to keep the peace.

In mid-September Grant sent General P. H. Sheridan to the Shenandoah. As soon as Early was defeated, Grant instructed, the valley was to be burned out so thoroughly that no future Confederate force could find haven there. Shortly, the young Federal general caught Early with forces separated at Opequan Creek "and won a most decisive victory," as Grant put it, "one which electrified the country." Striking hard with his 50,000-man force, Sheridan drove Early's 20,000 before him, pushing him through Fisher's Hill, Mount

Unable to collect $100,000 ransom from Chambersburg, Md. (below), Early's men burned the town.

Rebel Colonel John S. Mosby, commanded Partisan Rangers, who engaged in guerrilla warfare.

Confederate Brigadier Gen. Thomas L. Rosser's cavalry harassed rear areas of Sheridan's army.

The men beyond the stacked rifles in photo at left are Confederate prisoners of war, captured in the Shenandoah Valley. Sheridan captured 4,000.

Right, Union commander in Shenandoah Maj. Gen. P. H. Sheridan is shown with his staff. Left to right are Gens. Sheridan, Forsythe, Merritt, Devin, and Custer.

Right, this drawing depicts Sheridan's army following Early up the Shenandoah. After the Battle of Cedar Creek, the Federal Army was in control of valley.

Jackson and New Market. By September 25th, Early retreated out of the valley to the east. "Now one of the main objects of the expedition began to be accomplished," Grant said, "Sheridan went to work—what he could not take away he destroyed."

Early, with reinforcements, followed the Federals. At Harrisonburg, he poised his army to strike, but Sheridan moved out during the night. At Fisher's Hill Sheridan turned his cavalry back on Confederate horsemen and drove them back in "considerable confusion," as Early admitted. Confederates lost 11 cannon, and Federals pursued for miles before they turned back north. Sheridan camped at Cedar Creek at the base of Massanutten Mountain, and

left for a conference in Washington. Early's scouts checked mountain trails, and Confederate John B. Gordon led three divisions over them at night to strike the weak Federal left in conjunction with an attack by the rest of Early's forces along the valley floor the next day. The Confederates attacked, and Sheridan's army, with the exception of one corps, was routed. Within an hour weary Confederates slowed to rest, and Sheridan raced back on horseback from Winchester, 20 miles away. He rallied his men at dusk, and the Confederates broke before them. Thus ended the valley campaign. By the following spring most soldiers of both armies were fighting at Petersburg. •

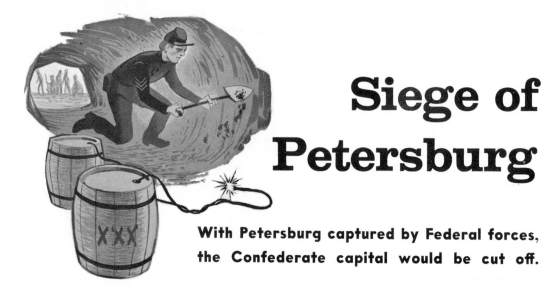

Siege of Petersburg

With Petersburg captured by Federal forces, the Confederate capital would be cut off.

AFTER the bloody repulse at Cold Harbor, Grant moved his army southeast around Richmond, hunting an opportunity to destroy Lee. "Lee's position was now so near Richmond," Grant noted, "and the intervening swamps of the Chickahominy so great an obstacle to the movement of troops in the face of an enemy, that I determined to make my next left-flank move carry the Army of the Potomac south of the James River."

By the middle of June, Federal advance units reached the James River, which flows southeast from Richmond. Two Federal ships, loaded with stone, were sunk in a narrow channel upstream to prevent Confederate gunboats at Richmond from coming down to hamper the Federal movement across the river.

Shortly, Grant's 115,000 soldiers joined their lines to those of Federal General Benjamin Butler's Army of the James with headquarters at Bermuda Hundred, the peninsula formed by the junction of the James and Appomattox Rivers, fifteen miles southeast of the Confederate Capital. Federal officers soon found rising spirits in their men. "When we reached the James River," Grant was pleased to report, "all effects of the battle of Cold Harbor seemed to have disappeared."

Butler's well-built base on the James served as a ready-made forward supply point to speed the Federal campaign against Confederates dug in before Richmond and Petersburg. Grant assigned Butler's army the task of holding the line around Bermuda Hundred and the Federal area north of the James, and assigned Meade's Army of the Potomac the mission

Napoleon howitzers, shown at left, were moved up to reinforce Grant's siege artillery at Petersburg. Widely used in both armies, these easy-handling and reliable pieces threw a 12-pound ball nearly a mile.

These sandbagged Federal Parrott "rifles," which for nine months bombarded Confederate lines at Petersburg (steeples on horizon), threw an 80-pound shot nearly five miles when elevated to angle of 35°.

This wooden building, at City Point, Virginia, was General Grant's headquarters in 1864. President Lincoln, along with cabinet members, visited here several times to discuss the political developments.

Below, the harbor of City Point, ten miles northeast of Petersburg at the junction of the James and Appomattox Rivers, was the principal base of supply for Federal armies which were besieging Petersburg.

The U. S. Military Railroad was vital to the Federal army besieging Petersburg. In previous campaigns the men were supplied by horse wagons (25 per 1,000 men), but muddy roads often halted these.

Below, artillery for the Federal army is shown at Broadway Landing on the Appomattox River, 17 miles south of Petersburg. This supply port was captured by Federal General Butler early in May.

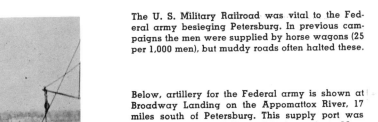

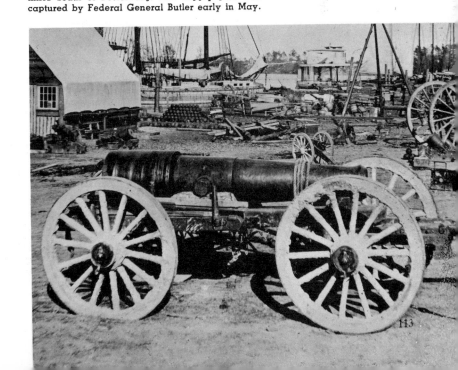

Shown above, at Bermuda Hundred, Virginia, is the headquarters of Federal Major General Benjamin F. Butler (inset). The soldiers are at work erecting tents for staff officers and digging drainage ditches.

On May 9, 1864, General William F. Smith's corps marched across this pontoon bridge, built by Federal engineers on the Appomattox River at Broadway Landing, to make first attack against Petersburg.

At right is shown a bomb-proof shelter at Bermuda Hundred, Virginia. Federal soldiers were quick to perceive the importance of maintaining covered works for protection from mortar and artillery fire.

Right, in an effort to provide a safe route from artillery fire and bypass river obstruction, Gen. Butler had his men dig a canal across Dutch Gap, a bend of the James R. It was never used by armed vessels.

Shown below is the Confederate battery Brooke, overlooking the James River below Richmond. This gun, and nearby pieces shelled the Federal forces while they were digging the Dutch Gap canal.

of surrounding the city of Petersburg, Va.

There was no room for brilliant maneuver here. Opposing armies dug trenches and hammered away. The tenacious Grant, aware of the deadly effects of his steady attrition against Vicksburg, determined to repeat the process here. While Grant's artillery bombarded and riflemen sniped in relative safety, deaths by disease outnumbered battle casualties. Entrenching was no longer the unpopular work it had been in earlier days. "The only benefit we gained at the bloody repulse at Cold Harbor," Grant observed, "was that the men worked cheerfully in the trenches after that, being satisfied with digging the enemy out."

Grant's supply base was City Point, a port on the James River able to accommodate deep-draft vessels. By early fall, 1864, a military railroad connected the river port with his Federal lines. Grant's supply build-up was unrelenting, even with detachments sent to defend Washington and reinforce Federal operations in the Shenandoah Valley.

One exasperated Confederate soldier

The thirteen-inch Federal mortar "Dictator," above, which fired a total of 45 rounds during the siege, could throw a 200-pound shot two miles. Recoil moved the weapon's rail-car emplacement back twelve feet.

Shown at left are Zouaves of F Company, 114th Pennsylvania Infantry, which participated in the siege. This photograph, taken near Petersburg in August, 1864, shows the distinctive uniforms of these troops.

Confederate Major General William Mahone, a Virginia Military Institute graduate, stopped the Federal attack at the crater which resulted from Federal mining operations under Confederate lines.

wrote home that it no longer did any good to shoot a Yankee since half a dozen new ones popped up to replace him. Although this was an exaggeration, the Federal army maintained at least twice as many men as did the defenders.

Yet, when the Federal trenches grew long enough to be measured by the mile, the supply of Federals to man them stretched until a single line of men had to suffice at some points. Federal officers wondered why Lee did not break through, but the Confederate leader had to make 60,000 men stretch along 35 miles of trenches.

Only once did Grant allow a radical attempt to interrupt his campaign of wearing down his opposition. In July, 1864, four tons of black powder were placed in a 500-foot tunnel under Confederate lines before Petersburg. Confederates had heard the digging beneath them and spread wild rumors.

One Federal officer recalled with satisfaction, "They said that we had undermined the whole of Petersburg; that they were resting upon a slumbering volcano, and did not know at what moment they might expect an eruption." Grant believed that the project would give handsome results, expecting "that when the mine was exploded the troops to the right and left would flee in all directions, and that our troops if they moved promptly, could get

These bomb-proof quarters at Fort Sedgewick were part of Federal-line fortifications before Petersburg. Confederate main lines were 1,500 yards away, but opposing pickets were only a few yards apart.

Forests were turned into bulwarks by both armies as a protection against enemy shelling. Confederate entrenchments were so strong they were not taken until final attack in the spring of 1865.

117

Union soldiers are shown waiting in the trenches before Petersburg as their officers walk the ramparts. At the time, beards were considered to be in style among soldiers, but most were too young to grow them.

Left, these young telegraphers performed a vital function for the army. Military telegraph lines connected Washington and City Point. Field headquarters were able to communicate with the front lines.

Right, this photo of Federal batteries before Petersburg was taken under fire on June 21, 1864, by Mathew Brady. An earlier attempt to take the picture was spoiled when Confederate shells exploded nearby.

Cannoneers of the 13th New York Heavy Artillery of Butler's army are shown in winter quarters at Bermuda Hundred, Virginia, 1864. These Federal artillerymen were waiting to be employed in the siege.

Federal soldiers are sniping from picket post near Fort Sedgewick, called by Confederates "Fort Hell." Fifty yards away are rebel pickets in front of Fort Mahone, termed by Union soldiers "Fort Damnation."

Shown at left is a wounded Federal Zouave being comforted by his companion in a campsite near Petersburg. During the Civil War more than 318,000 Federal and 271,000 Confederate soldiers received wounds

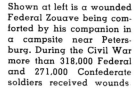

This dead Confederate soldier was photographed two days after he was killed in the Petersburg trenches. Confederate defenders, overwhelmed by F attacks, had no ti bury their fallen com

120

in and strengthen themselves before the enemy had come to realization of the true situation."

The explosion did not take place on schedule owing to a break in the fuse. This was remedied by volunteers who crawled through the shaft to relight the fuse. The mine finally blew at dawn on July 30th. "Suddenly the earth trembled under our feet," wrote a Federal officer. "An enormous mass sprang into the air. A mass without form or shape, full of red flames, and carried on a bed of lightning flashes, mounted toward heaven with a detonation of thunder. It spread out like a sheaf, like an immense mushroom whose stem seemed to be of fire and its head of smoke."

Federal soldiers began running to the rear, fearful that the debris would fall on them, but were soon rallied and the attack started forward. The advancing Federals found "an enormous hole in the ground about 30 feet deep, 60 feet wide and 170 feet long, filled with dust, great blocks of clay, guns, broken carriages, projecting timbers and men buried in various ways—some up to their necks, others to their waists, and some with only their feet and legs protruding."

Shortly, dismayed Federal officers found their attack stalled again when their men broke formation to rush for a look into the awesome hole. "Before the brigade commanders could realize the situation," reported one Federal officer, "the two brigades became inextricably mixed, in the desire to look."

The attackers were re-formed and again started forward into the hole, and up its far side. There, however, they found themselves under fire from the rear as Confederates rushed in along the trenches from both sides. The crater had become a trap instead of an entrance. The attack cost the Federal army nearly 4,500 men. Confederate General Mahone reported over a thousand Federal troops taken prisoner when his men drove the remnants of four Federal divisions from the crater that afternoon. The Confederates lost 1,000.

"The effort was a stupendous failure," was Grant's disgusted comment, "and all due to inefficiency on the part of the corps commander, and the incompetency of the division commander who was sent to lead the assault."

After the mine experiment the main purpose of Grant's army was to extend itself around Petersburg to the southwest to cut the rails and roads which supplied Lee's army. As Federal trenches were dug south in the fall and winter of 1864, Confederate trenches were kept apace, and vicious fights at their ends prevented significant movements past them. Short probes by both sides were attempted and thrown back, as Grant continued hammering.

By spring, 1865, Lee found that he had to break the Federal line before him in order to move his dwindling Confederate army south in relative safety. On the night of March 25, 1865, "Confederates, under pretense of surrender," reported one Federal soldier, "approached the scattered pits (before strongpoint Fort Haskell) simultaneously, and, after a short parley, pounced upon their would-be benefactors and disarmed them to a man."

Most of Fort Haskell's defenders were playing poker inside a dugout as the infiltrators signaled companions forward. "A hundred men now passed in to the guns and went prowling about, silencing with noiseless knife or bayonet every man they could find awake or asleep."

As Confederates filed through the breached line, a nearby Federal strongpoint opened its batteries upon them and at dawn Federal riflemen finished the destruction of the ill-fated attempt led by Confederate John B. Gordon. The Confederates fell back and the siege ended. •

Photograph at right shows Confederate soldier fallen among chevaux-de frise, a defense made of sharpened spikes inserted through timbers and used in the same manner as modern barbed wire. The devices were employed by both armies and were effective in providing portable defenses against surprise attacks from foes.

121

Sherman's Marches

A great military success was needed to re-elect Lincoln, continue the war, and save the Union.

Kenesaw Mountain (below), which lay astride Atlanta's approaches, was scene of battle between Sherman's forces and those of Johnston, June 27.

"IT IS only those who have neither fired a shot nor heard the shrieks and groans of the wounded, who cry aloud for blood, more vengeance, more desolation—war is hell." With these deeply reflective words, General William Tecumseh Sherman later described the great conflict in which his was the grievous task of splitting the Confederacy east to west, just as Grant had split it north to south at Vicksburg.

In early May, 1864, Sherman led 100,000 Federal troops southward from Chattanooga. Flanking the 43,000 rebel troops under Johnston, Sherman fought toward Atlanta, Ga., a hundred miles away. After sharp battles at Tunnel Hill, Dalton, Re-

saca, and Dallas, he finally reached Kenesaw Mountain, a natural obstacle "honeycombed with rifle pits and bristling with cannon," as a Confederate described it. Sherman assaulted directly from the front. Confederates opened withering fire which caused 3,000 Federal casualties without military gain. Shifting back to his flanking tactics Sherman marched columns around the Confederates to threaten the Atlanta Railroad behind Johnston, and the Confederate general was forced to move his forces into the Atlanta fortifications.

The incensed Southern populace demanded Johnston's removal because of the constant retreat, and President Davis re-

Gen. William Tecumseh Sherman is shown below in a dramatic pose on horseback within a captured rebel fort near Atlanta. Inset at right shows front view of this 44-year-old major general.

Federal Major General John A. Logan led an assault by the Fifteenth Army Corps against Kenesaw Mountain on June 27.

Below, Atlanta was evacuated during Sherman's occupation and became a Federal military center.

Shown above is an on-the-spot drawing which depicts the fierce struggle atop Kenesaw Mountain.

Photograph above shows Federal troops within a recently-captured Confederate fort near Atlanta.

placed him with John B. Hood. "Sherman and I," said General-in-Chief Grant, "rejoiced when we heard of the change. Hood was brave and gallant, but unfortunately his policy was to fight the enemy wherever he saw him."

Taking advantage of Hood's penchant for bold attacks, Sherman tightened his lines around Atlanta and prepared for the expected sally. It came within a week. Confederate General Hardee's attacking troops surprised a Federal corps resting at noon on July 22nd, but soon collided with another Federal corps astride its route. This action, the Battle of Atlanta, developed into a vicious hand-to-hand struggle. By

Replacing Johnston as defender of Atlanta was impetuous Confederate General John B. Hood (below).

the end of the day Federal General Logan's men counted over 1,000 Confederate casualties in front of their corps alone, and Logan's men took a like number of prisoners, including a Confederate general. Leaving part of his army to bombard the city, Sherman turned south against the railroads supplying Atlanta. Hood was forced to abandon the city and place his Confederates between Sherman and the 34,000 Federals held at the Andersonville prisoner-of-war camp. Sherman then occupied the city without opposition. "Atlanta was ours and fairly won," the general reported. Victory had an exhilarating effect in the North, for the city was the last industrial site of significance in the deep South.

Emptying occupied Atlanta of its residents, Sherman prepared for his march to

On the night the Confederates evacuated Atlanta, they blew up six engines and 100 cars of munitions.

This Federal picket post, near Atlanta, was midway between main U. S. line and advance guards.

View below looks down the Confederate line around Atlanta after its capture by Sherman.

Above, after Sherman captured Atlanta, he ordered defenses built against rebel forces outside city.

Above right, Federal Major General James B. McPherson was killed in Battle of Atlanta at age 34.

127

Shown above are Federal wagon trains leaving Atlanta at beginning of Sherman's march to the sea.

Below, this is how the Federal line at Nashville looked on second day of the battle for that city.

Upon leaving Atlanta, Sherman's men demolished rail terminals (above), storehouses and factories.

Savannah on the Georgia coast, a march in which he planned to cut the South in two. But while Federal troops gathered in Atlanta, Hood struck the Atlanta-Chattanooga railroad, hoping to turn Sherman out of the city. Nevertheless, Sherman held on while moving 65,000 men north in pursuit of the raiding Confederates. Hood's men struck the Federal forces of General Corse at Allatoona Pass where the railroad cut through a sharp ridge, but Corse defended vigorously to protect the million and one half rations stored there, while Sherman hurried reinforcements. "I am short a cheek bone and one ear, but am able to whip all hell yet," Corse semaphored to his approaching commander. Before Sherman arrived, the Confederates swept north to wreck twenty miles of track above Resaca, Ga., then turned west and halted before Gadsden, Ala.

"That devil Forrest," as Sherman termed Confederate General Nathan Bedford Forrest, wrecked Federal rails and supplies in Tennessee. After destroying six million dollars' worth of Federal supplies near Nashville, Forrest joined Hood's approaching forces and took charge of Confederate cavalry.

Sherman sent General Thomas to Nashville to block Hood, a move which brought on the battle of Nashville, December 15th and 16th, with the consequence that the Confederates were routed to the south. Forrest fought off the Federal pursuit until

The railroad terminal in Nashville was an important depot of U. S. Military Railroad system. Four railroads radiated from here.

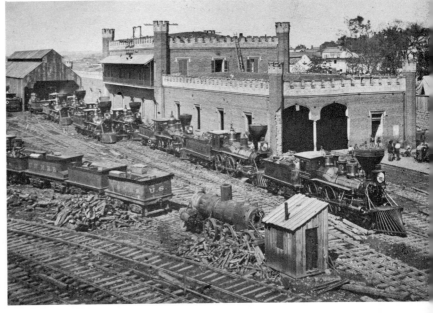

his troops crossed the Tennessee River in north Alabama. With Hood occupied in Tennessee, Sherman began his march to the sea on November 13th, leaving Atlanta in flames. Sherman left no forces in the city, and determined to provide his army with supplies from the countryside during the 300-mile march. "We have cut adrift from our base," wrote a Federal staff officer, "the history of war bears no similar example, except that of Cortes burning his ships."

One of the Federal "boy generals," Hugh Judson Kilpatrick, swept the front for the marchers with his 5,000 cavalry, opposed only by an insignificant number of Confederate horsemen under Joseph Wheeler. The latter's riders found that "every rice and grist mill was burned, as well as cotton gins, barns of corn, and fields of potatoes destroyed." A Tennessee cavalryman said that he saw "time and again, long rows of dead horses numbering from 30 to 150. Upon taking every mule and horse that the citizens had, they would kill their own, not leaving the citizens as much as a half-dead mule." Sherman prepared a note to be mailed to his wife at first opportunity. "They regard us just as the Romans did the Goths, and the parallel is not unjust.

Many of my stalwart men with red beards and huge frames look like giants."

Sherman's men wreaked a hundred-million dollars' damage in Georgia, only a fifth "of which inured to our benefit—the remainder was just simply waste and destruction." The march was Sherman's supreme moment. He wrote proudly of Negroes "simply frantic with joy. Whenever they heard my name, they clustered about my horse, shouted and prayed in their peculiar style." By Christmas Sherman possessed Savannah and the forts encircling it, and prepared to sweep north through the Carolinas. "Somehow," Sherman observed, "our men had got the idea that South Carolina was the cause of all our troubles, and therefore should fall on them the scourge of war in its worst form."

Turning north in January, 1865, Sherman brushed aside scattered Confederate cavalry detachments. Charleston and Fort Sumter were evacuated by Confederates as Sherman bypassed them inland. Confederate Wade Hampton, a native South Carolinian who had fought with Jeb Stuart in Virginia, commanded defenders at South Carolina's capital, Columbia. By February 16th Sherman stood on the river bank opposite the city. "Thank the Al-

Cavalry of Gen. Joseph Wheeler (above) was Sherman's chief opposition during march to the sea

Above, during his march to the sea, Sherman made a path of destruction sixty miles in width.

Right, Gen. Nathan Bedford Forrest is credited with saying, "Git thar fustest with the mostest."

These members of 21st Michigan Infantry marched with Sherman through Georgia and the Carolinas.

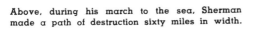

On Feb. 16, 1865, Sherman ordered shelling of Columbia, S. C. (above). The city was destroyed by fire.

General Hugh Judson Kilpatrick was commander of Sherman's cavalry during the march to the sea.

Rebel Lieutenant Gen. Wade Hampton led Southern cavalry against Sherman at Columbia, S. C.

Shown below are Federal artillerymen in captured Confederate Fort McAllister, which guarded the Ogeechee R. approaches to Savannah, Ga.

mighty God," a Columbia Negro said, "Mister Sherman has come at last, Mr. Sherman has come with his company."

After shelling the city, Sherman sent part of his army through it. Stored cotton bales promoted the spread of fire and the city became a mass of flames. "Even if peace and prosperity soon return," Sherman wrote, "not for a century can this city or state recover. It is not alone in the property that has been destroyed, it is in the crushing downfall of their inordinate vanity, their arrogant pride."

By early March Confederate Joseph Johnston was restored to command in the lower South, and he gathered remnants—some 15,000 men—in mid-March for a defense at Bentonville, North Carolina. Two days of battle there brought the same disheartening order to Confederate soldiers, "Withdraw," and Johnston backed his men through Raleigh. While a truce held his opponent in place, Sherman brought up additional strength. Realizing the futility of further fighting, Johnston conferred with President Davis in Greensboro, N. C., and met Sherman on April 26th at a farmhouse to terminate hostilities. •

Below, this 8-inch Columbiad is shown being removed by Federals from captured Fort McAllister.

133

End of the Confederacy

After four years of anguish the limit of endurance was reached; men returned to their homes.

Below, the Capitol of the Confederate States, across the James River at Richmond, was one of the few buildings to escape heavy damage in fires that followed city's evacuation by the rebel army.

AT the beginning of 1865, the outcome
was clear. The Confederate army before Nashville had been wrecked and
chased below the Tennessee River into
Alabama. Sherman was marching to join
Grant. Sheridan had swept the Shenandoah. Lee's army in the Petersburg-Rich-
mond lines was melting away from Grant's
increasing pressure.

On March 26th Lee notified Jefferson
Davis that Richmond could no longer be
defended. If Grant pushed his line farther
westward it would curve north and cut off

Ruins of the Gallego Flour Mills in Richmond ex-
emplify the South's ruined industry at the close of
the Civil War. Federal armies seized main industrial centers and paralyzed South's war capacity.

After Richmond was destroyed by fire during night of April 2, 1865,
witnesses called the conflagration the worst of the war. Exploding
magazines in rebel arsenals rained shell fragments on fugitives.

Shown at left are Federal horses hitched to a fence among the smoking ruins of Richmond. Federal cavalry, arriving on April 3, 1865, comprised first Union forces to enter the Confederate Capital.

Above, a Federal soldier of the occupying forces is shown amidst the rubble of the gutted city. Troops stacked their arms and, drafting all able-bodied men found in the city, heroically battled the flames.

Left, these captured Confederate guns, taken at Richmond after the city was abandoned, were parked on the wharves of the James River, prior to their shipment to the national arsenal in Washington, D. C.

any possible withdrawal along the Appomattox River. Three days later Grant sent Sheridan galloping westward. Lee hurried George Pickett and Fitz Lee after him. The two Confederate commanders entrenched at Five Forks where Sheridan struck them late in the afternoon of April 1st. "The signal was given," recalled a Federal, "and the concealed (Federal) infantry, many thousand strong, sprang up and advanced by echelon to the right. Imagine a great barn door shutting."

When the Federal barn door slammed shut, the Confederate Army of Northern Virginia had received its worst beating of the war. Sheridan took 5,000 Confederates prisoner.

President Davis was in a Richmond church the next morning, Sunday, April 2nd, when Lee sent him a note that Richmond and Petersburg must be evacuated. That afternoon panic swept through the populace. The arsenals were fired that night by evacuating Confederate troops.

A Federal officer climbed to a hill outside the city to see what he described as "the grandest and most appalling sight that my eyes ever beheld. Richmond was literally a sea of flame, out of which the church steeples could be seen protruding here and there, while over all hung a canopy of dense black smoke, lighted up now and then by the bursting shells from the numerous arsenals."

General Robert E. Lee sat for this Brady photo in Richmond a few days after his surrender. On the left is his son, G. W. C. Lee, and on the right, Colonel Walter Taylor.

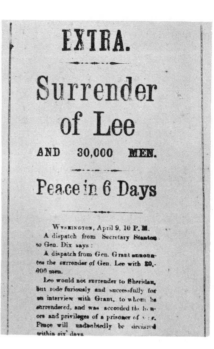

EXTRA.

Surrender of Lee

AND 30,000 MEN.

Peace in 6 Days

WASHINGTON, April 9, 10 P. M.
A dispatch from Secretary Stanton to Gen. Dix says:

A dispatch from Gen. Grant announces the surrender of Gen. Lee with 20,-000 men.

Lee would not surrender to Sheridan, but rode furiously and successfully for an interview with Grant, to whom he surrendered, and was accorded the honors and privileges of a prisoner of war. Peace will undoubtedly be decided within six days.

On May 24, 1865, the Grand Army of the Republic marched in a victory parade, the "Grand Review," down Pennsylvania Avenue in Washington.

Lee's forces retreating westward in an attempt to elude pursuit before turning to the south, found their way blocked at Appomattox Court House by Sheridan's cavalry and infantry. With no supplies or hope for further resistance, Lee answered Grant's surrender demand: "I reciprocate your desire to avoid useless effusion of blood, and therefore . . . ask the terms you will offer."

"Whatever his feelings," Grant said of an impassive Lee upon meeting him, "they were entirely concealed from my observation; but my own feelings, which had been quite jubilant on the receipt of his letter, were sad and depressed. I felt like anything rather than rejoicing at the downfall of a foe who had fought so long and valiantly."

Ironically, the two Generals-in-Chief met each other shortly after noon on April 9th in the living room of a local house-owner, McClean, who had moved from the Manassas area in order to get away from the war.

After exchanging pleasantries Lee suggested they get on with the business at hand. Grant sat down to write out the surrender agreement. "When I put my pen to the paper," Grant said, "I did not know the first word that I should make use of . . . I

only knew what was in my mind." It was a simple letter instructing Lee on the terms extended. Lee wrote a memo agreeing to them.

About three o'clock Lee shook hands with Grant and left. "He mounted his chunky gray horse," said a witness, "and lifting his hat as he passed out of the yard, rode off toward his army, his arrival there being announced to us by cheering, which as it progressed, varying in loudness, told he was riding through the bivouac of the Army of Northern Virginia."

Lee's 28,000 men were paroled to their homes. Five days later Sherman paroled 37,000 of Johnston's in North Carolina. By the end of May most Confederate forces in the West surrendered. The Confederate President, defiant to the last, was captured in Georgia and imprisoned for two years.

The Confederate States and its army, born in conflict, died in the echoes of its final battles. The Grand Army of the Republic, less 359,000 dead on the battlefields behind it, made its last military campaign in May, a "Grand Review" down Washington's Pennsylvania Avenue. The nation had its rebirth as Lincoln had promised in his famous address at the Gettysburg cemetery. The states were again united. •

Civil War Soldier and Weapons

Federal soldiers were better equipped than Confederates.

THE Civil War soldier was young. Over two thirds of Federal soldiers were under 22, while about 800,000 were less than 17. Most soldiers came from farms. Nearly one fourth of Confederates and about five per cent of Federal troops were foreign born. These were mainly German, Irish, and Scandinavian. About 200,000 Negroes served in the Union Army, and a like number were hired as laborers. The Confederate army had a few Negro soldiers but none saw combat. Federal soldiers, with a few exceptions, wore blue issued uniforms. Confederate uniforms varied from gray to blue or brown according to his source of supply. At the

Scene at left shows Federal rifled muskets stacked near the Petersburg railroad station at end of the war.

Above, many regiments had special identifying features on their uniforms, such as the leggings of these Federal Fourth Michigan Infantry troops.

Below left, such photos as this 3¼″ by 3½″ ambrotype of a young Federal soldier were popular during the war. Ambrotypes (on glass) and tintypes (on metal) were cheap and could be made in minutes by photographers who visited camps. To the right is Private E. F. Jennison from Georgia, killed at Malvern Hill at age 16. Below him is another teenage Rebel. Boys often swore they were "over 18" by writing that number in shoe.

141

Shown below are Federal rifles: 1—U. S. Rifle-Musket, 1855 model, .58 caliber, 56″ overall; 2—U. S. Rifle-Musket, 1861 (same data); 3—U. S. Rifle-Musket, 1863 (same data); 4—Remington, 1862, .58 cal., 49″ overall.

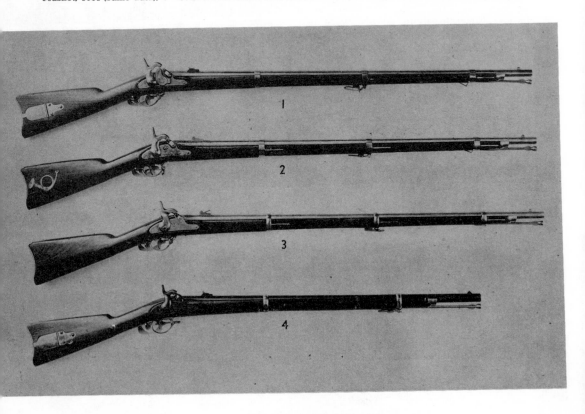

Confederate soldiers wore motley uniforms which were mostly products of the community from which they came. There was more uniformity in Federal army.

Confederate arms: 5—Palmetto Musket, .69 caliber, 58" overall; 6—Richmond Rifle Musket, 1863, .58, 55¾"; 7—Cook Infantry Rifle (copied from British Enfield) .58, 49"; 8—Morse Musket, .70, 57".

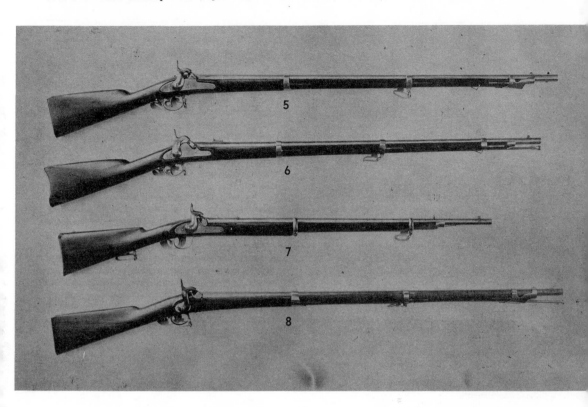

beginning of the war, some soldiers of both armies wore gaudy militia outfits such as red baggy pants of Zouaves and yellow apparel of Confederate "yellowjackets." The forage cap with sloping flat top was typical in the East. Confederates wore the hat generally.

Federal infantry companies comprised up to 82 privates, while Confederate companies included about 125. Although Federal regiments were organized for a strength of about 1,000 men—Confederate for 1,400—few regiments of either army maintained over half strength. Federal privates in infantry and artillery were paid $11.00 monthly in the beginning; the cavalry troops received one dollar more. This was increased gradually to $16.00 by 1864. Confederate privates began at the same rate, but it was increased to $20.00 by 1865.

A canvas forage bag, 12" by 8" by 3", was the soldier's pack, but a blanket roll often sufficed. Paper cartridges were carried in a cartridge box on the belt or shoulder strap. The cap box held percussion caps. The canteen was of wood or metal. The typical Federal weapon was a rifled musket. The Confederate carried a Springfield or Enfield smoothbore musket, often a flintlock converted to the percussion system. The rifled musket, which weighed about 9 pounds and cost $20, was fairly accurate at 100 yards. Many soldiers purchased the 16-shot repeater, the Henry rifle or carbine, for $35, and some Federal units were issued repeaters late in the war. Forty rounds of ammunition was the standard issue to a soldier. Cavalrymen and officers usually did carry pistols. Officers, artillerymen, and sometimes cavalrymen carried swords or sabers.

The basic Confederate food ration was cornbread, field peas, and occasionally sweet potatoes. The Federal ration was hardtack crackers and white beans. Salt pork and fresh beef were issued when available. Cattle on the hoof accompanied both armies.

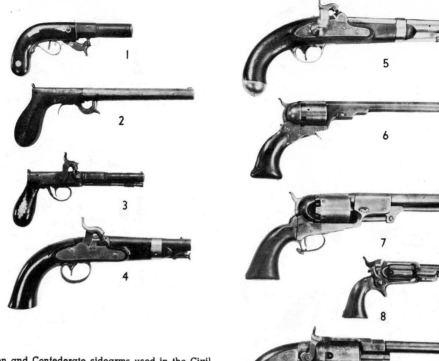

Union and Confederate sidearms used in the Civil War: 1—underhammer pistol, Robbins, Kendall and Lawrence, Windsor, Vt.; 2—underhammer pistol, made by a Cherokee Indian at Qualla Town, S. C.; 3—pistol, B. Fowler, Hartford, Conn.; 4—pistol, U. S. Navy, 1843; 5—pistol, Henry Aston, Middletown, Conn.; 6—percussion revolver, Colt, 1836; 7—revolver, Colt, 1849; 8—percussion revolver, Colt, 1855; 9—revolver, Wesson and Leavitt.

Shown below are bullets picked up from Fredericksburg battlefield. The calibers range from .32 to .70.